“Is it about

# "Is it about that boy?"

## The Shocking Trauma of Aversion Therapy

A memoir by

Jeremy Gavins

Published by JGSCR Publishing



A CIP catalogue record for this book is available from the British Library.

ISBN 978-1-9996819-0-6

Book layout and design by Clare Brayshaw

Cover design by Sarah Cowan

Prepared and printed by:

York Publishing Services Ltd
64 Hallfield Road
Layerthorpe
York YO31 7ZQ

Tel: 01904 431213

Website: www.yps-publishing.co.uk

# Contents

*It was a snowstorm. Whiteness was falling in huge flakes, beginning to settle on top of the icy road, on top of my shoulders, my head. That's why I didn't wait in our usual place. I stood on the far side of the road, under the shelter. The bus didn't come and I began to shiver. The traffic was as heavy as the snow – nobody could see the way ahead. That's why he didn't see me at first. It's why he didn't see the approaching vehicle ...*

CHAPTER ONE

# Just Jeremy

## Me and my dad

"If a snail is crossing your garden and it has got six feet to go to get to the wall, and it travels half the distance left every hour, how long will it take to get there?" asked my Primary School teacher. I raised my hand almost immediately, saying I knew the answer. The teacher told me to write it down and bring it to him. A couple more boys did the same; then he asked me to read out the answer. I said, "It will never get there."

It didn't matter how close the snail got to the wall, because in the next hour it would only cover half the distance left and though this distance got shorter every hour, it would never get there. The teacher praised the three of us, saying that, at only ten years old, we had the brains for difficult mathematical concepts about infinity and we'd be good at maths.

I rushed home, eager to tell my dad. He was an engineer, brilliant at maths and I thought he'd be pleased with me. When I told him about it, he lifted his right hand and, prodding my neck with his index finger, his exact words were,

"You've got a dirty neck, go and get it washed." No praise, nothing. He completely blanked me and offered no encouragement. I was just a ten year old in need of some appreciation, but I was snubbed. I have never forgiven him for that response. It was carved with a blunt chisel into my brain.

In 1953 three events happened. Everest was topped, the Queen was crowned and I was born. In the life that followed, I would go on to top many mountains. I could also have become a queen, but society had other ideas so it was not to be. In gay slang, queen is a term used to refer to an effeminate gay man. I think the main reason I would not go on to be a queen was that I was born into a Catholic household. The fact that it was Catholic didn't mean anything to me for the first sixteen years of my life. So long as I went to church often, confessed my sins, said my prayers and served my time as a good little altar boy everything went all right. Then I fell in love.

My parents were Bert and Betty. I have three brothers, the oldest Donald, then Neil and Alistair. I was brought up in the north of England in a town called Keighley in West Yorkshire.

As I grew up, I thought my dad and I were two very different people. It would take me a lifetime to realise we were in fact very similar. He was a soldier in the Second World War. He fought his way across Europe and into Germany. The many horrific sights he'd witnessed I can only guess at. He never talked about them to me, so I had no way of knowing what he went through.

I, on the other hand, was just an innocent homosexual boy growing up in a Catholic man's world. I too, learnt to hide away my innermost thoughts, much to my own detriment. Who knows? Maybe if he had been a bit more forthcoming and open about his life, a little of that would have rubbed off on me and we could have talked to each other. The only time I did talk to him about my sexual feelings he snubbed me again, not for a dirty neck this time, just as a person who had robbed the word 'gay' of its meaning for him. We never talked again about anything other than the mundane.

The last time we met before he died, we didn't speak, as I could still see that sneer in his face that he used when he looked at me. To him, I was still the sinful queer boy, and to me, he was the man who represented everything I hated about the Catholic religion.

I'd often tried to impress him, but it was hard work. He was such a jack of all trades, a perfectionist. I thought if I couldn't get any praise from my dad, I'd have to search out other people who would appreciate me. My maths teacher was certainly a good influence on me as maths became my favourite subject. My teachers were happy for me when I did well, so my schoolwork improved too. It was no coincidence that my class teacher wrote in my end of year school report: 'Jeremy has made good progress this year. An interesting boy too, and very helpful.'

## Losing my yellow tie

I was eleven when I lost my yellow tie. Losing my yellow tie was the most important event of my life so far. It was associated with the first time I was naked and touching another naked boy. Of course, I had been naked with other boys in changing rooms many times but apart from looking, I never touched them.

In those days every child in the neighbourhood played outdoors. Most of the time there'd be a big gang of us playing football or just charging about in the park, climbing trees or throwing sticks at the grey squirrels. One day while I was having a pee behind a tree in the park, Martin, a boy a few years older than me, came over and watched me. He got his willy out and started playing with it. I was intrigued, so I watched him. He asked me to get hold of his willy, which I did, readily. Nobody had ever asked me to do that before.

A few days later, I met Martin and he took me to an old barn in some fields behind the park. It was dark inside and had a musty hay smell. Martin opened a shutter, letting the light reveal a messy mix of old motor parts, hay and other rubbish. It felt warm inside, which was perhaps as well because, as I was wondering what was going to happen next. Martin beckoned me to the back of the barn. "It will be quiet here, Jeremy, no-one will see us," he said. "Let's take all our clothes off." We both stripped off, and he encouraged me to touch him, and as I explored his body, he had his hands all over mine. It felt good to have his hands on me. It was a beautiful experience. My first sex. It was lovely.

When I got home, I was still in a dream world, until my mum said,

"Where's your yellow tie, Jeremy?"

Oops, I'd forgotten to put it back on, I'd left it somewhere in the barn.

"I took it off to play football," I told her. "I'll pick it up tomorrow."

When I returned the next day to look for my tie, Martin helped me look for it. Throughout my life, I've never bought a tie. I have borrowed them occasionally for job interviews. I couldn't see the use of them from a clothing point of view, and no tie would ever come close to being as memorable as my old yellow one.

In addition to visiting the barn, Martin and I would strip naked in a local woodland and run about like a couple of nudists, playing together. I used to see Martin every so often until, being older than me, he went off into the world of work and we lost touch.

My general attitude to life was going well at this time, and my improvements at school meant that I passed my 11+ exams, allowing me to go to an All Boys Grammar school. I could hardly wait.

## Sore bottoms

I started at St Bede's Catholic Grammar School, the day before my twelfth birthday. The school was in Bradford, ten miles by school bus from Keighley. If I missed this bus, I had to catch an ordinary one and walk up Emm Lane, a long steep hill, to school. This meant I would be guaranteed to be late, leading to some form of punishment, usually lines of the format, "I must get out of bed earlier and catch the school bus," a few hundred times. Many a day began by sprinting down my street into town, stuffing a jam butty into my mouth and just managing to get on the bus before it left.

I thoroughly enjoyed being at my new school. I was not the thickest of the bunch but low to middling. When I began school, I started playing rugby as well as football. Having a rather stocky body meant I was better suited for rugby. I also preferred rugby as I could throw myself about in the mud and have to spend more time naked in the showers with the other boys as we scraped the mud off.

In second year swimming, one of my mates, Dave, pushed a boy into the pool and the teacher made him bend over, with just his trunks on. He gave him six strokes of his strap as we all watched. After class, Dave said to a few of us, "Do you want to see my bottom?" We went in the toilets, and Dave dropped his pants, revealing a very red striped bottom. I said to him, "Gosh that must have hurt, can I touch your bottom?" It turned me on as he allowed me to feel his bum. I noticed that he'd got a lot of admiration for taking the strap so well, without crying out. I thought that is something I could get into, so always tried to take my punishments as quietly as I could. This was not always possible.

During an English class, a boy returning to his seat, tripped over my outstretched leg and the teacher called me to the front. As I approached his desk, I noticed he had already taken out his leather strap. Twenty inches long, a quarter inch thick and two inches wide. I'd seen it before many times and knew what was coming next.

"You know the drill, Gavins, right hand out." He said.

I held my right hand out, palm up and supported it with my left hand gripping my wrist. Then the teacher brought the strap down with a loud "thwack" which hurt like hell.

"Change hands."

No time to hesitate, left hand up supported by my now throbbing right, he brought the strap down again. 'Thwack,' followed by, "change hands."

It was very painful. After the fifth stroke, I found it hard to open my left hand for the last stroke, the teacher stood up, told me to bend over and gave me a hard one across my bottom. Of all the forms of punishment I received, I hated being strapped on my hands, the throbbing pain would last for ages. I preferred it on my bottom.

One day I accidentally smashed a window in a classroom. I'd thrown a wooden blackboard duster at a mate; he ducked, and the duster went flying through the window. I was sent to see the Deputy Head. After the usual telling off, he gave me the choice of either being banned for two weeks from the school bus or receive the strap. To be banned from the school bus meant that, to arrive on time, I would have to catch an earlier bus. Having to explain to my parents why I was getting up earlier than normal would have lead to more punishment at home, so ideally I would have chosen the strap.

However, this teacher was renowned for having a bigger, thicker and longer strap than anyone else; I knew from past punishments just how much a couple of strokes hurt. So this time I went for the bus-banning option. Unfortunately, he then said, "Well Gavins, if you are more frightened of my strap than a bus ban, then it's the strap you are going to get." The Deputy Head told me to come to see him in his study at one o'clock, after my dinner.

As I walked along the corridor to his study, I could see that there was another boy, Tony, waiting at the door. We both looked at each other, grimaced and, reluctantly, I knocked on the door. The Deputy Head gave us six very hard strokes of the strap apiece. They were delivered one at a time each whilst we were looking at each other, bending over either end of his desk. It was torment as he walked from one of us to the other. He'd made punishing boys into a fine art. I think he enjoyed it. The sound of our punishment was easily heard outside the room, and some of my classmates thought I had received all twelve strokes. When I told them I had, they wanted to inspect my bottom. Unfortunately Tony told them we'd got six apiece and I was mobbed by the boys, laughing and pushing me around. Despite my very sore bottom, I enjoyed the experience immensely.

### A queer boy

As a teenager, I used the words queer, puff and homosexual to describe myself. This was in the late 1960s. It wasn't until I was twenty, that the word gay came to be regularly used.

There was one boy, Tom, who liked to masturbate in the park with me, but I knew he wasn't queer. All he talked about was girls and what he would like to do to them. When he got a girlfriend, whom he later married, he kept saying to me, "Don't you think she is gorgeous Jeremy?" He kept talking to me like this until I'd had enough of it and asked,

"Do you do to her what you talked about when we were wanking in the park?"

"Of course I do, wouldn't you?"

"Er ... no Tom, I prefer to have sex with boys rather than girls."

He looked at me. "Are you queer?" he asked.

"Yes, Tom, but you had better not tell anyone about me, or I will tell people what we used to do in the park together."

He avoided me after that, but he didn't reveal my secret. He did invite me to his wedding, just so that he could tell me once more how lucky he was to find such a beautiful girl. I thought she was quite dull, but then what did I know?

When I was playing with Martin, to get to our barn, we had to go past the public toilets in the park. I sometimes noticed men hanging around them. I asked Martin about it, and he just said that's where the older men go and do what we were doing. He warned me off going there saying it was dangerous. Once, ignoring Martin's advice, I went to see what was happening in the toilets. I met a young man who wanted to touch me up. I enjoyed it. But I didn't go again as I thought most of the men there were rather old, hairy and smelly.

In the Scouts, I found more outlets for my sexual feelings. When I was fifteen on a scout camp, I noticed one of the young scout leaders had been watching me. When he beckoned me into his tent, I joined him. He took all my clothes off and enjoyed himself with my body. Camping trips often lived up to their name.

I thought at least these men appreciated me, unlike my dad who always found fault. I don't believe it had any harming effect on me. It felt good, and I liked the compliments I received from these young men. These days this would all be called child abuse, but how could it have been abuse if I enjoyed it? I couldn't get enough of it. The form of child abuse I did suffer from, was that of being brought up in a family environment where to show love was taboo, and all sex was bad.

CHAPTER TWO

# Learning to hide

### Patience

In my teens, I began to notice that my parents thought having sex was a sin. When the family were sitting in the living room watching telly, if my dad saw any sex on TV, he would get up and turn it off saying, “Why do they always spoil the programmes with this filth?” This sex was the ordinary stuff between men and women. There were hardly any homosexuals on TV in those days but when there were, my parents said they were evil and sinful.

My dad treated wildlife type programs on TV the same way. It was seen just as disgusting to watch any pair of horses, spiders, dogs, sheep or anything having sex. They thought David Attenborough was a pervert. My dad’s version of Noah’s Ark would have had the animals going in one by one. It wasn’t just sex that was bad, any form of closeness was taboo too. I don’t think I ever saw any closeness between my parents.

So there I was, with my parents watching actors pretending to love each other on TV, being told that what I was seeing was wrong and sinful. I had to find some way of being able to sit with them, but ignore what they were saying. I’d get out a set of playing cards and, with a wooden board on my knee, I’d play forms of solitaire patience. I invented a couple of patience games that could go on for hours. I found that I could just ignore what they were saying and play with my cards. I learnt to sit in my own world and ignore what was going on around me.

I couldn't understand why wanting sex was so wrong. I didn't have any guilty feelings about what I was doing. According to my parents, all sex was bad. My desire to be with boys was equally as bad as my mates wanting sex with girls. I think the only difference was that my friends never stopped talking about it, whereas I got the feeling that it may be best if I didn't.

On most Sundays, there was the weekly parental row. I cannot remember what they were about; it was just a time to make myself scarce. Shouting "Abyssinia," (I'll be seeing you) I'd run out the back door into the street and freedom. I don't think I ever loved my parents. I am sure my parents did love each other, I just wish they had made it more obvious. I didn't hate them; I was just sort of neutral.

### "God's good"

My mum was okay, but my dad was always pointing out my wrongdoings or criticising me for something or another. They were always fair-ish and never violent towards me, apart from a beating with a piece of wood a few times when I was naughty. Somehow they were not there, distant, not around when I needed them. If I did want to discuss anything with them, they always found a reason not to talk about anything helpful. Usually, it came down to them pointing out my persistently dirty neck or hands. I began to believe they may have loved my body (just the clean bits mind) but had no time for the person living within that body.

My parents were so into their God that whenever I did anything right, they would give God the praise for showing me the right path. “Deo Gratias,” I was told so many times I got sick of hearing it.

But *whenever* I did anything wrong it was never anything to do with God. It was always me that was to blame.

I do have to thank my parents for two things. One, was that my mum taught me how to cook. When I was fourteen, I won first prize at a Women’s Institute cake making competition for my Victoria sponge. The other far more beneficial thing, was that nearly all of our holidays were in the Lake District. Walking with the family was always a bit of a bind, but I found pleasure walking miles in the mountains on my own, doing my own thing, going my own way, with no-one else to bother me.

At age sixteen, when we were staying in Ambleside, I set off early for a walk on my own, saying I’ll be back later. I went up to Black Fell above Tarn Hows, fully intending to turn around at this point and go back, but something felt good inside me and I found the mountains beckoning me on. I found my way around Lingmoor, over Pike O’Blisco, along Crinkle Crags, Bow fell, Rossett Pike, Sergeant Man, and then down Blea ridge to Loughrigg and back into Ambleside. A distance of about 25 miles. I got back to a telling off at about 11 o’clock at night. Ah the wonders (and fitness) of youth.

One of the most annoying things about my dad was that he didn’t like to spend money. I think he liked to see money accumulate in his bank accounts. All the family felt sure he had alarms fitted to the electric and gas meters and could tell if anyone in the house dared to use any. While the rest of the family were freezing to death in various parts of the house, dad worked away in the cellar using up copious amounts of electricity on whatever he happened to be making at that time. He never changed either. When both my parents were in their eighties he still wouldn't allow my mum to turn the fire up, even though the cold was making her ill. When she was offered a place in a nursing home, she couldn't get away from him fast enough. She was at least warm for the last few years of her life.

Dad was an expert DIY person. No job was too big for him. A skilled car mechanic, electrician, plumber, carpenter, decorator, engineer. It helped that he had a few slaves, erm sorry ... sons, to help him. He would often call out for me to help him with his car. I spent many hours lying underneath it, bleeding brakes, adjusting things, my dad shouting, "The other way, idiot," at me for turning the brake-bleeding nut the wrong bleeding way. It was no wonder I had a magnetic attraction for dirt. It was a family joke that all his sons had to spend their time listening for squeaks and noises in various parts of the car as we drove along. Later in life when I tried to do any work on my own vehicles, I had great trouble trying to work out which way to turn a nut and often tightened things up when trying to undo them. When working under my vehicle, I had to make a drawing of the direction to turn a nut and take it under with me.

My dad was brilliant at everything, and of course, I was useless at everything and if I ever felt I was good at anything it was always 'God's good doing' of course. Eventually, I found something I was brilliant at, working outdoors, building dry stone walls. I could be as muddy and mucky as I liked.

When my parents told me they loved me, I knew they didn't. It wasn't the real boy that they loved; it was the outer face; the 'normal' never had sex with anyone, just the good little altar boy. Not the hidden away daydreamer who was always wishing he was somewhere else.

I didn't know the meaning of love. But I did know the meaning of hate. They said they hated homosexuals but loved me. If they found out that I was a queer, would they still love me? I very much doubted that. It would be safer for me to keep everything hidden. I slowly built a mental wall between the inner boy and the outer self. When stuck at home with my parents, I found that I could get out my cards and retreat behind my wall into the mountains.

### "Well done son."

My teeth grew crooked from an early age. They didn't bother me, but they did my parents. Throughout my childhood, I had many visits to a dentist in Keighley. This particular dentist was a bit of a torturer, who liked to have you in agony while he drilled holes through everything. On one visit I told this dentist that I had a bad cold and I might need to cough. He ignored me, so when I did cough he drilled straight through my tongue. Blood and bits everywhere. He didn't say sorry; he just told me off for moving. I hated him and was scared of going to the dentist.

When I was twelve, it was decided that I needed to get my teeth straightened out properly. So, for some unknown reason, I ended up going to a dental hospital in Leeds for treatment. It was probably free. My mum always took me on the train.

The first time I went, I had to sit on a kind of babies' high chair. Sat up high, the various dentists could peer into my mouth while standing up. They prodded around inside my mouth for a while. Then one of them filled my mouth with metal plates that fitted over my teeth. There followed a lot of faffing about as the dentist pushed and pulled this metalwork in and out of my mouth, until he found the right size. Then the plates were filled with a blue paste and shoved back in again. The blue stuff had to be bitten into until it set, twenty minutes or so. They would use the impressions to fit braces to my teeth to straighten them out.

When this started, I was told to breathe through my nose. But, despite the warning, I couldn't help gagging as I attempted to breathe through my mouth. This lead to a nightmare of coughing, gagging and spluttering while one of them dragged the plates out of my mouth. Scooping out the blue gum, he told me off for trying to breathe through my mouth. He imprinted two thoughts in my mind, I don't like this man and how do I escape?

It took a real effort to calm down and breathe gently through my nose. Using the same technique as I used when sitting at home with my parents, I learnt to dream that I was in the mountains and not stuck in a chair trying to withstand the discomfort. It was the only way I could endure it, forcing myself to be calm, slowing my breathing down and imagining I was walking in the Lakes. Definitely not thinking about what was going on in my mouth.

One of the dentists was a good-looking young man with black hair, and I always tried my best for him. One day after he took the plates out he said, "Well done son, you did really well there. Are you all right?"

"Yes, Dad, I'm fine, thank you." I quickly answered.

I loved the way he smiled at me. My mum told me off for calling him dad, but I was quite chuffed. "Wow!" I thought, some praise for doing something right for a change.

According to various diaries, I attended this dental hospital in Leeds forty-two times over five years culminating in three nights in a hospital when I was sixteen. I had fourteen visits to the Keighley torturer as well. I hated dentists, unless they were good-looking. All this teeth straightening didn't work. I solved some of my crooked teeth problems myself. Some of them were kicked out playing rugby and a few more went when I was gay-bashed in my twenties.

At school, my education was going along quite nicely. There were no problems according to my reports for the first three years. Always the same stuff, must try harder, needs more effort, but also comments like: "Jeremy has a very pleasant disposition and has a good approach to work and games." and "works very consistently and makes good progress." These positive remarks continued to the fourth year when my reports started to deteriorate.

"Has no sense of urgency."

"I hope Jeremy will cast off his rather peculiar attitude to authority ... Not that he is actively hostile, just totally non-co-operative," wrote my class teacher.

"Needs to work harder," wrote my religion teacher.

I was a happy homosexual boy but the steady drip, drip, drip of negative comments about homosexuality spouted by my parents and television had begun to work on me. I know that they said people like me were not normal, but the feelings I had for other boys my age felt normal to me. I was scared of anyone finding out that I was one of 'them.' I had to protect my inner feelings somehow.

At the tender age of fifteen, in the company of most people, I had to be seen as the rugby-playing, church-going, good Catholic boy on the one side. On the other, behind a wall of secrecy, was the homosexual boy well hidden. My outer persona as a straight boy had to be kept at the front at all times. I learnt to be vigilant. I am not saying that the two parts of me weren't happy. I was still a happy queer, but only on the inside.

I had many boyfriends in and out of school, but they were mostly platonic. I had to be very careful to make sure that I didn't reveal my inner child. I never had any girlfriends. I kept well clear of girls as I felt nothing for them. I looked at some boys and often wished one would make the first move like Martin did. I just wanted to find another boy like him. But how could I tell if I found one?

CHAPTER THREE

# Stephen

## A beautiful face

As the new classes were being sorted out for the fourth year in September 1968, I glanced around the room to see who was in my class. I noticed a new boy. He had the most beautiful face I'd ever seen in my life. He looked a little like the singer Donovan but far better looking. Black curly hair and a lovely kissable nose. I don't know, I have a thing about noses. He was stunningly gorgeous. The rest of his body was good to look at too, slim and fit, with bony hands.

Listening to registration, I found out his name was Stephen. I thought he would be just another of those to be fancied at a distance but this boy was somehow different. Although Stephen was in my registration class, apart from Religious studies, English and French, we took different subjects, myself sciences, him languages.

We didn't really meet socially either, as I was the straight macho rough rugby player and I thought he was a bit arty farty. I couldn't take my eyes off him. At one point as I stared at Stephen, he looked straight back at me and smiled with a twinkle in his eyes. I nearly fainted, I couldn't believe how beautiful he was.

I managed to bump into him entering classrooms and chose any innocent chance to be near him. I held myself back though, I didn't dare do or say anything weird to him. I was frightened of scaring him away. Through the next couple of years, we became mates. I slowly started to spend as much time with him as possible, which was a bit difficult as we lived miles apart. He lived in Bradford and we didn't meet up during the holidays in those first two years. Just at school.

Unfortunately for me again, because Stephen wasn't into outdoor sports I never had the pleasure of seeing his naked body in the showers. Perhaps as well because I am sure it would have been impossible for me not to hide my hard-on. In the fifth year, with the help of my new-found friend, I managed to turn around my negative attitude at school.

At the end of term July 1970, I passed five 'O' Levels: English, Maths, Biology, Physics and Chemistry and a grade 1 French CSE. I have to thank Stephen for helping me pass the French exam. He would speak to me in French which I then had to learn to find out what he was talking about. He made me respond to him in French so, after struggling with my oral French over the previous four and a half years, I passed.

The holiday period from July to September 1970 was a long summer of yearning to see Stephen. In my diary on July 2nd, I wrote: "Can't wait for September when I will see S again."

I took on my first ever proper jobs that summer. The first was at a wood mill. I only lasted a week before I got sacked. My job was to collect timber together on pallets for the orders that came in. I was paid piecework which meant the faster I made up an order, the more I got paid. On the Friday as I was making up an order, a wagon came in and parked right in front of my pallet. I asked the driver to move it but he said: "Not 'til I've 'ad my break."

I thought I'll just have to wait and having nothing else to do I wandered off and lit up a fag. I'd started smoking at fifteen. The foreman spotted me and told me to get on with my job. I went back to find the wagon was still there. Without thinking too much about it, I climbed into the cab, saw the keys in the ignition, started the wagon and moved it forward about ten yards, turned it off and left it there. This wasn't the first time I had driven a vehicle, having had a go in one of my dad's friends Landrover a couple of times. Then I went back to work. When the driver came back he said:

"Who moved my wagon?"

"I did because you were too idle to move it for me," I said. So he went and told the manager and I got sacked. I should have lied and then it would have been OK. The trouble with me is that I would often speak quickly and tell the truth, when I should have thought about it first and lied. This wouldn't be the only time I lost a job due to my outspoken manner. I did however, get paid thirteen pounds seven shillings and six pence for the week. My second job was a clerk's job in the accounts office of an engineering mill. An easy job which earned me eight pounds eight shillings and seven pence a week. I just did the job for two weeks. I'd never been as rich.

### My breath of fresh air

When I first saw Stephen again at school on the 9th September 1970, I couldn't resist running to him, pulling him into an empty classroom and whispering in his ear:

"I think you are the most beautiful boy in the world ... I love you."

To my joy he turned to smile at me and gave me a hug, saying,

"About time, Jeremy, I thought you were straight."

He wasn't shocked, he didn't run away, and he didn't call me queer. Though we were not with each other every day, I realised that I had at last found another boy who thought like me and would be my boyfriend. I wished I had told him earlier but I was afraid he would reject me.

The day after I told Stephen I loved him, I wrote in my diary:

"I have stopped writing my diary now cos I am in love and going mad," followed by "I love SCR," which were Stephen's initials. Followed by, "Not gonna write my diary no more 'cos it will be all about S and I don't want my mum to read what I feel."

When I was out walking alone in the Lakeland fells I felt fit, well and happy. Often walking through the hills I would rejoice in just being out there. I felt I was meant to be there. Part of something far larger than just me. Sweating hard and feeling hot I would occasionally be subjected to a cooling breeze which felt good.

A breath of fresh air, my whole body and spirit felt alive, transcendental. I was walking as one, without having to hide my secret side. I could shout out loud my joy and often did. I never got these feelings when I was walking with other people. This could only ever happen if I was on my own. I could be totally relaxed not having to hide my emotions. Stephen was my breath of fresh air. Being with him made me feel good; keeping me together, calming my fears and warming my spirit. I did not have to use my straight side. This alone was quite refreshing. I could just be the whole me.

When I was alone with Stephen, I was always the soppy one. Stephen was nearly a year younger but in many ways, he was much more life experienced than me. I think my family upbringing had held me back in growing up. I had lived half my life just hiding away ... Wishing I was somewhere else. Once when Stephen caught me staring at him he said:

"I wish you wouldn't do that, Jeremy."

"What? What am I doing?"

"Sometimes you make it so obvious, staring at me like that."

"I can't help it, I just find you so beautiful. I love every little thing about you."

"That's OK, but we've got to keep our love a secret. If anyone finds out we'll be fucked."

So we had to learn to be just mates when in groups, which was difficult for me but had to be done. We had to be careful at school not to let anyone else into our secret world. I just adored him and it was me who wanted closeness. He didn't resist me when I wanted to touch him. I think we'd both lived in a frightening world without feeling or tenderness for so long that just to be able to relax our guards with each other was fantastic. He was my confidant. We lived in our own little world within a world that would vilify us if they knew our secret.

## The Middle C

Stephen had a middle name that started with a C. When I asked him what it stood for, he wouldn't tell me. He said he hated his middle name and didn't want me to use it. I cajoled, nudged, and I kept trying to guess it and often came up with new names to try out, but he said I'd never guess.

"Cecil?"

"Nope."

I loved being outdoors so much, that when I had to decide which 'A' levels to take, I wanted to go for a Forestry or Earth Sciences degree. So I wanted to do 'A' levels in maths, chemistry and biology. But my dad was never going to let me do biology, and told me that I should go into engineering or the textile industry. "You'll always find work in those industries," he said.

That meant I had to do maths, physics and my dad allowed me to do chemistry, as it had become my favourite. Then he discovered that a new subject called Engineering Science was being offered as well as physics. My dad told me to go for it. Unfortunately, I was the only one who chose it. I hoped it would get cancelled, and I could do biology, but the school decided to go ahead with it, with just me and the teacher. This teacher just happened to have one of most boring, monotonous voices possible. With no one else to confer with, or copy from, I couldn't see why other people thought it would be such a good idea for me to take it by myself.

Stephen didn't do any of my A levels, so we were only together in the same class at registration, use of English and religious studies.

"Claude?"

"Nope, now Claude I'd have no bother with, you'll never guess."

At school at the start of term, I had a falling out with the rugby coach and gave up playing for the school. A friend on the school team, Nigel, suggested we try out training for Bingley Rugby Union Football Club. I started training for them. My first game for Bingley was on 31 October 1970 when I played prop forward in their Colts team. I then played every Saturday for the rest of the season. I enjoyed playing for Bingley. The set up was far more organised than school rugby. Plus, of course, they had a clubhouse with a bar. I usually played for the Colts, but would occasionally play in the 'B' team. On the 13th March 1971, I had the pleasure of playing against my brother, Neil, when Bingley played my hometown club, Keighley. We won 22-3.

## Coming Together

Stephen introduced me to Diana Ross and, making sure no-one was watching, we used to sing her songs together. I can more or less date my relationship with him by her song albums. Diana Ross in June 1970 with songs like 'Now that there's you,' 'You're all I need to get by,' and my favourite 'Ain't no mountain high enough.' In November 1970 as our friendship was blossoming, the album 'Everything Is Everything' came out with the songs: 'Close to you' and I will always remember Stephen dancing down the school corridor towards me singing 'Doobedood'ndoobe, Doobedood'ndoobe, Doobedood'ndoo.' Then in July 1971, there was the album 'Surrender,' with 'I'll settle for you.' One song we both loved singing, and it still makes me smile to this day when I sing it out loud was 'Come together' with its lovely thoughts of cumming together.

"Christian?"

"Nope, you must be fucking joking, Christian would be terrible, but it's far worse than Christian!"

I was totally in love with him. He was always trying to wind me up, teasing me. Flirting, making sexual remarks and innuendos. Calling me, "Jeremy the Sugar Puff Bear."

From 1957, Jeremy the Bear was the advertising face of Sugar Puffs, and on the advert, his theme tune was "If You Go Down In The Woods Today." So throughout my childhood, I had to put up with people calling me Jeremy the Sugar Puff Bear. Ha-ha, little did they know.

Stephen knew all he had to do to get me going was to smile at me with his sparkling eyes. He would stand in one of the sixth form study cubicles, hidden from view and I would stroke his bottom. We did kiss, hold hands, sang songs together, smooched, danced, went to parties and even went to gay pubs together. Just to have him close meant so much to me. He was such a lovely person. The absolute happiest I'd ever been. Apart from masturbating, we didn't have sex; there was no need. Sex with Stephen was not important to me. With my closeted family home life being so loveless, it was lovely to be hugged by someone who did it knowing full well what I was.

"Cabel?"

"Nope."

We were very careful to keep things well hidden. I am sure a few of the boys knew but no teachers or parents and brothers. Like me, he was the third son of his parents. He never came to my house, and I never went to his. He only lived ten miles away as the crow flies but since buses can't fly it was nearer to fourteen miles. We just met at school, or he would come down into town occasionally on a bus as I came in on a train. There were two gay pubs in town, but it was dangerous to go there too often.

The Junction was the most well-known, but we only went there a couple of times. We had to be very careful, because even though homosexuality had been decriminalised in 1967, it was still illegal for men to have anything to do with anyone under twenty-one. It was ridiculous that I could quite happily get a beer at age eighteen, but I could only have sex with women legally.

"Cain?"

"Nope."

"I'll keep trying you know, I will find it somehow."

"I told you, you won't guess it. The only way you'll discover what it is, is if I tell you."

Our lives went along outside our relationship. I went fellwalking whenever I got the chance. I would walk over Ilkley Moor in all weathers. We were a dog owning family, Cairn and Airedale Terriers mainly. I would often get away from being at home by taking a dog out. From our house, it was a ten minutes walk to the first park. Then, past the yellow tie barn, into the second park, across the main road into the cemetery. Using the golf course bridge to get over the river Aire, we'd cross the golf course and over a canal bridge into Howden wood. The path climbed steeply through the wood to the fell road and finally onto Ilkley Moor. There we would roam free across the miles of heather moorland.

**C is for ...**

Stephen was quieter spoken, almost always calmer, or more in control than I was. His kind of team was to be on the School Entertainments Committee. We played alcoholic's chess occasionally with our mates. This was the same as normal chess but with the pieces replaced by alcoholic drinks. The pawns were halves of beer, rooks and knights as pints of lager or beer and all the rest of the pieces as shorts. There were limited places we could play this game, as we needed not only a table big enough to set out an eight by eight set of beer mats, but also an understanding landlord. Then the game commences and as pieces were taken, whatever the drink, it must be downed when taken. The game always started seriously, and it always ended in a silly game of 'take' until we all fell down in a drunken laughing heap on the floor. In 1971, after decimalisation, the cost of two chess teams; sixteen pints of beer and twelve shorts, including doubles, amounted to about £3.20. In 2017 the same round would be over £80.00.

Money was often easy to find as, on the bus to and from school, there were always one or two card games going on, three card brag and poker at which I excelled. I would often double my dinner money. Putting our knowledge of maths to good use, a few of us even set up a bookies so the boys at school could bet on horses.

Finally, in September 1971, Stephen told me his middle name was Carmel.

"Wow!" I said, "You're right Stephen, I'd 'a never come up with that name. Isn't it a girl's name?"

"That's why I hate it."

"Can I call you Stephanie from now on?"

"Only if I can start calling you Jeremy the Sugar Puff Bear again."

He thumped me on the arm and started singing, "If you go down in the woods today, you'll be sure of a big surprise, 'cos Jeremy will be bare down there, having my cock for a picnic."

"Oooh ... Carrrrmellll."

"Well now I've told you, Jeremy, you must promise never ever to use it again in my presence, or I'll never talk to you again. I hate it."

I never did use it, but the knowledge of it would become vital to me later in life.

In December 1971, I sat my mock A-level exams. These were meant to be a trial to see how we would do in the real thing the following June. I got my results in January. I passed all of them. In my school report at that time the teachers said of my chances of passing my A-levels in the summer were:

'Very good all round result, Jeremy should get at least a B.' From the chemistry teacher.

'Jeremy is working quite well and has the ability, if he keeps up the progress he will pass.' From the maths teacher.

'I shall be satisfied with nothing less than a C in the summer." From the engineering science teacher.

These reports show the state of my mind. I was doing OK. I was very happy having Stephen around. It made my school time very enjoyable. I believe that because of my relationship with Stephen, I had managed to keep going with all my A level work. I went for an interview at Leeds University to study Chemistry and was offered a place if I got two D's for my A levels. I also applied to go to Camborne Mining College in Exeter and again would be accepted on getting two D's.

Life just went on wonderfully, and I built a big thick wall of secrecy around my relationship with Stephen. If I was ever asked by anyone about my relationship I stonewalled them. I loved Stephen for his total and absolute unconditional acceptance of me. I had never experienced this from anyone before. I just loved Stephen for being Stephen. I wish I could find the words to describe him adequately. I felt proud to be with him. I felt so starved of love and acceptance from my family that I came to rely on his presence.

But of course, all great things come to an end. I think a natural end would have happened to our relationship if I hadn't been so dependent on Stephen for the love in my life.

CHAPTER FOUR

# Diseased

## My first breakdown

Towards the end of March 1972, Stephen and I went to a party in Leeds. It was just a quiet get together with some of our friends. We were sat on the floor just relaxing in the friendly ambience, smoking dope. We started talking about the future.

"We've had a lovely time Jeremy, but by July we'll probably be going our separate ways."

I suddenly realised that he was going to leave me. I was distraught.

"How will I survive without you?" I realised that after school finished this summer, I might not see him again and I didn't want him to leave me.

He said, "You'll be all right, we'll keep in touch."

Back at school, the hidden part of me was worried about our relationship ending. I felt awful. I didn't know what to do. We didn't live in each other's pockets, and during school time we didn't see each other all the time, but I knew he was never very far away. The end of school just never dawned on me. I continued to stress myself out. I couldn't talk to anyone else about our relationship. I couldn't discuss why I felt so rotten. There was no one to ask for help. I was so obviously suffering, but no one asked me why. Stephen did his best to keep me going, but I was getting depressed and going down fast. The wall which protected my inner queer self was falling apart.

What I did next was the worst mistake of my life. It was a moment of weakness I would regret forever. Everything that happened to me after this point was a result of my inner wall not being tough enough to contain my feelings.

I was in a maths class when, without asking for permission, I just got up and left. I didn't have any plan. I just needed some air. I didn't know where to go. Leaning against the wall in the corridor trying to decide what to do, which way to go, I failed myself utterly and slid to the floor, crying. A teacher walked past and, noticing my condition, asked:

"Are you all right, Gavins?" I mumbled, "No."

"Come with me," he said and, head down, I followed him down the corridor to his study where I collapsed onto a chair. I'll always remember that chair. It was one of those antique low-backed Captain's chairs with curved wooden side arms to hold. I sat forward, head down as I held the arms tightly to stop me falling. The teacher asked me why I was crying. I told him I was in love and he said: "That's all right, everyone falls in love." He was considerate and sympathetic and asked, "Why are you crying about it?"

I confessed: "Because he's called Stephen."

I told him about Stephen and my love for him and everything else. I just couldn't help myself. It all came tumbling out. It was just a relief to talk. He listened for a while, and when he spoke again, his mood had changed completely. He said I was abnormal, sick and ill, a disgusting sinful boy. The problem for me was he wasn't an ordinary teacher, he was a Catholic priest.

I told this person what was going on in my head, and I know I should have kept quiet about my homosexuality, but

I didn't realise what I was doing. I just wanted someone to put their arm around me and say you'll be all right. Perhaps I was naïve to think I'd get any sympathy and understanding.

The priest took me to see the Headmaster, a Monsignor, who asked me how I felt about being a homosexual. He too told me that I was sick, that homosexuality was a terrible disease. I couldn't stop crying. I just wanted some sympathy, but I didn't get any. They just made me feel even worse.

The Head then told me to go home, "You must not tell your parents about this. Think of the shame it would bring on your parents to find out they have a homosexual son." I was too trusting; young for my age and vulnerable. I needed some comfort. But all I got was more pain. I was an abnormal, diseased homosexual.

When I got home, I just said "Hi" to my mum, quickly changed and went straight out again to the pub, which was always my answer to any of my problems. Get drunk.

I had to report to the Head or another priest every morning when I came to school. They then allowed me to go to class. I had to report to them at my breaks too. The priests would question me about my homosexual feelings. They endlessly told me that I had a disease; that I was sinful. Wherever I was there always seemed to be a priest around watching me. They wanted me to go into detail about what Stephen and I did together. I do not think they believed me when I said we didn't have sex. When some of my friends noticed my behaviour, I couldn't tell them anything. I just fobbed them off.

And where was Stephen in all this? The school had banned me from seeing him at school; I don't know, maybe he was going through the same hell as I was. I didn't see him for a while. Maybe he was avoiding me. I feared that I had dropped him in it. I didn't want him to think I had betrayed him. I hoped with all my heart that he didn't hate me for letting our secret out.

At one point I did get free of my minders and went to find him. He was in one of the sixth form study cubicles. Before I had the chance to say anything he handed me a piece of paper on which he had written out for me the first lines of the Diana Ross song "Reach out I'll Be There." This version of the song is slightly different from the Four Tops song as it includes the phrase "Reach out for me ... Boy" instead of Girl.

So I did. I reached out for him, and I knew he was all right with me. He told me he was called in to see the Head but just told them it was all a load of bollocks and he was not queer. I think the different way they treated me was because I was eighteen and he was only seventeen.

**Options, or the reason I later found it so hard to make decisions.**

The priests at school convinced me that I was a sick, diseased boy. I felt ashamed to be me. I learnt to recognise the look of disgust on the faces of the staff as they knew I was a sinful boy. I knew that I was a homosexual and therefore I must be diseased; my teachers keep telling me this so it must true. I am queer, liking boys rather than girls. I wouldn't have had to keep things secret if I was normal. I didn't know it was a disease.

This brainwashing went on for about two weeks. I was just in a perpetual daze. I tried to concentrate more than ever in my classes, to keep my mind off what was going on. I reckoned that the only way out of my situation would be to pass my exams and get away from school, my family and all this turmoil by going to university.

One day I was taken to see the Head again, and I thought here we go, more misery. I know I am diseased but why couldn't they just leave me alone. As I stood in front of his table, he looked up at me and said "I am afraid you only have two options. You can carry on as you are and in that case, we would have no alternative but to expel you. We will inform your parents why we are expelling you. Think of the shame you will feel when everyone finds out that you are a homosexual. We will expel you immediately, and you will not be allowed to take your A levels."

*Fuck,* I thought. I knew the news would devastate my parents and who knows what my dad would say or do to me. From his usual behaviour when homosexuality was mentioned, I knew he would kick me out. What would have happened to the other things I enjoyed doing? Playing football and rugby, would I lose all my friends?

Without taking my A levels, I wouldn't be able to go to University. I already had no-one to turn to, would I be able to see Stephen again? I was confused and knew that people would hate me if they knew the real boy. I just wanted to be loved, hugged and accepted. So when Stephen came into my life, I adored him for just allowing me to be me. No need to be on guard when in his company and I could be completely relaxed.

"However ... you do have another option," the Head continued, "We can stop you feeling like this, we can heal you of your disease. If you agree to go to the doctors, we will not have to expel you or tell your parents. You needn't tell your parents about this because when you're cured, you've no need to tell them anyway." And I never did.

He said that they could cure my disease if I went to my GP and asked for the treatment. The school couldn't send me for treatment. He told me to go and tell my GP that I was a homosexual and I wished to be cured.

I didn't think I had a choice. I did, but I was too young to know. I went to see my GP on Mon 15th May 1972. I asked her for the treatment to cure my homosexuality. My GP didn't try to talk me out of it. She just confirmed that homosexuality was a disease and she readily agreed to my request.

CHAPTER FIVE

# "Good, it's supposed to hurt."

## Dr Grumpy

A week after seeing my GP, I received a letter asking me to attend an appointment at Lynfield Mount Mental Hospital in Bradford on June 1st. I wondered why it was at a mental hospital as opposed to my local hospital. I thought if you had a disease you would be treated in an ordinary hospital.

I was called in to see the Head, who asked if I had received an appointment. When I told him I had, he said I should come into school normally that day and someone would accompany me to the hospital.

When I went to the hospital for the first time, the priest I'd first spoken to walked with me to the hospital. He told me that it was so that I would know the way when I had to go on my own. I was surprised to find that the looney bin was just a fifteen-minute walk from the school. We left by the back gate of the school, up Leylands Lane, across Toller Lane, then all the way to the end of Duchy Drive, across to the front entrance of the hospital. A walk I would be making many times during the next six months.

I was apprehensive, but assured by the priests and teachers that this was the only way to be cured of my disease. When I first entered the hospital, I was taken to a room and had to stand at the front of a big black table. Sitting at the other end was a man. I took an instant dislike to him. I did not like his abrupt attitude. Why some men assume that all homosexuals want sex with any man amazes me. I thought this doctor was a grumpy horrible little man. He told me he was a psychiatrist. He asked me lots of questions.

"How are you feeling, Jeremy?" he said

"I am not sure how I feel, apprehensive, I suppose."

"Do you like your parents?"

"Not particularly, I put up with them."

"What do you think of your religion?"

"What the fuck has my religion got to do with this?"

He ignored what I said and continued "Do you masturbate, Jeremy?"

"Yes of course I do, doesn't everyone?"

"What do you think about when you are masturbating?"

"When I'm on my own or with someone else?"

"On your own?"

"I think about having sex with my school mates."

"Do you want to go out with a girl?"

"No."

I didn't meet many girls apart from relations, and I certainly didn't fancy any of them. He asked about my homosexual relationships.

"What are your preferences? What kind of men do you like?"

I told him that I'd had sex with a few boys, and young men. I didn't say anything about Stephen as I hoped that I could keep Stephen out of this. I thought that if I could keep Stephen secret from this chap, I could keep my love for him. I didn't want to stop loving Stephen.

"How do you feel about the way you have been treated recently at school?"

Well, I thought, I had been deprived of seeing Stephen, been talked to in a disgusting manner by the priests and the

Headmaster, so I was not in any mood to say anything good about anyone. So I didn't.

"I am angry about what has been happening to me and also angry about having to be talked to and examined by everyone."

"Do you want to be cured of your disease Jeremy?"

"Er, yes, I suppose so."

"You don't sound convinced."

"No, I want to be cured. It's just all happening so quickly."

He said that homosexuality was a terrible disease and if I followed their treatment programme they would cure me of it. I agreed to it because I didn't have any choice. He said the treatment would consist of me receiving electric shocks when I had homosexual thoughts and thereby associating the pain with being homosexual. This would stop me desiring males. He said it was called aversion therapy.

The thought of getting electric shocks was frightening, but I just supposed that they knew what they were doing. The doctor didn't say anything about how the treatment would make me sexually interested in women.

In 1998 I had a mental breakdown and was diagnosed with depression and post-traumatic stress disorder. I asked my then GP to see if there was anything in my medical records relating to the time I was at the mental hospital and the AT. The following is a quote from my medical health notes written by the psychiatrist at the time deduced from our one and only meeting before the treatment started.

> *'This boy has homosexual desires and fantasies ... He is truculent, resistive in the interview situation, antagonistic towards his parents, antagonistic towards his schoolmasters, antagonistic towards his church and*

*generally discontent. He has both heterosexual and homosexual fantasies, but the homosexual tend to be dominant. He has masturbatory guilt both related to his religion and external to his religion ... What we should do at this stage is to try and avert him to his homosexual fantasies by aversive techniques and by operant conditioning encourage his heterosexual desires ... And I will continue to see the boy with a view to trying to help him psychotherapeutically as far as his personality disorder is concerned.'*

As I walked back to school, I tried to forget all about it and think about my exams. The first day of my A level exams was the following Monday, 5th June, taking Chemistry. I was a bit down about all the things that had happened over the last couple of months, but I was determined to do my best still. I filled in the whole paper and thought I had done OK.

**Tuesday 6th June**

I had an appointment at the mental hospital at 9.30. I walked from school on my own. After reporting at reception, a man in a white coat took me to some changing rooms. He told me to strip naked and put all my clothes in a locker.

"Put some of those on," he said, pointing towards some dressing gowns and slippers. Usually, I would have been aroused being told to strip off by a man, but this was completely different. I could feel the disgust in his voice. He said I should take my watch off too, and put it in the locker. I could feel his eyes following me as I took my clothes off. None of the slippers fitted me, but I quickly covered up my nakedness with a gown. Leaving the changing room, I followed him down the corridor, flip flopping in my loose slippers, until we came to a door. He turned to me and said, "When you come for treatment, you have to go to the changing rooms, strip off, put on a dressing gown and slippers, report to this therapy room door and knock." He knocked and opened the door for me.

I entered into a small room with a rather high ceiling. There was just a table, two screens and a couple of chairs. One of the chairs was a wooden one with a straight back with armrests. On the table were a pair of slide projectors. There was another man in a white coat here, a doctor, I assumed. I hadn't seen him before. He did tell me his name, but I can't remember it. He just looked at me and said, "Take off the dressing gown, fold it, place it on this chair," the straight-backed one, "then sit on it, with your arms on the rests."

The doctor then fastened both my wrists to the arms of the chair, using a pair of leather straps. Then he picked up a grey band that had two metal buttons on one side and a pair of wires coming from the other. The wires snaked across to a box on a table. The band was attached to my right forearm. I felt very exposed sitting naked in front of him as he worked around me. He told me that I had to look up at the screens and obey his commands. "I am going to test the electrodes to make sure they are working."

I felt a terrible stabbing, burning pain in my right forearm arm. I couldn't stop from being surprised by it. I tried to pull away from the pain, but I couldn't escape it. He asked me if it hurt and when I said yes, he said, "Good, it's supposed to hurt." The doctor then explained that I was to look at the screens in front of me, and on one screen would appear pictures of men and on the other women.

He placed a switch in my left hand, saying if the pain got too much I should flick the switch, and the picture of the man would change to a picture of a woman, and the electric shock would stop.

Then the slide show began with pictures of mainly naked men, either solo or having sex and as I looked up at them, an electric shock was applied, sometimes coupled with a buzzer. The initial shocks were very painful, and over time they seemed to get stronger. I learnt that my left-hand switch didn't always work, and I would continue to be shocked at the same time as frantically using the switch. Now and then there would just be a picture of a naked woman. When they showed me a picture of a woman, the shocks stopped. The only sounds were the clicks of the projectors, the buzzer and my gasps of pain as the shocks bit into my arm. No words were spoken apart from just once when at one point I looked away and shut my eyes, but the doctor said: "Watch the screen, Jeremy."

Then suddenly the screens went white, and the doctor came across. He undid the straps, told me to go and get changed, and he would see me at my next appointment. Short, abrupt, no conversation. As I put the gown back on, I noticed it was soaked with my sweat. When I looked at my watch in the changing rooms, I was surprised to see that well over an hour had passed.

I left the hospital in a daze with my mind in confusion as to what had just taken place. I didn't have much time to sort it out though, as I had my second 'A' level exam at 1.30 that afternoon. It was my first maths exam. I sat at my desk, opened the exam paper, wrote my name and just sat staring at it. I couldn't think. I tried to get up and leave, but one of the teachers said I had to stay at least thirty minutes. After half an hour, I just got up and left. Some people watched me go, but no one said anything.

When I got home, it was easy for me to go and hide in my bedroom. I told my mum I just needed to do loads of revising and not to disturb me. I couldn't revise, though. I couldn't sleep either.

Wednesday's exam was the second half of Tuesday's maths exam at 9.30. I turned up, sat down and wrote my name and address. I looked at the questions, but I couldn't think of anything. I then wrote essays about each of the questions. To answer a question about levers I wrote a story about Levers Water, a tarn in the Lake District. I asked for so much extra writing paper that some of the teachers came and looked over my shoulder to see what I was writing. I was there in body but not in mind. At 11 o'clock I got up and left, went straight across the road to the pub and got drunk.

The next day I had my second chemistry exam. I tried, but I was too worried about what was going to happen on Friday. After leaving the exam room, I went to see the Headmaster. I told him I couldn't concentrate on my exams and could he delay the treatment until my exams had finished, but he was insistent that the therapy had to continue. I should've stopped the treatment, but I was too scared of being expelled.

**Fri 9th June**

I attended my second session of aversion therapy (AT) at 9.30. It was the same as Tuesday. I shivered, not with the cold, as I changed into a gown and with my flip-flop loose-fitting slippers, I shuffled my way down the corridor to the door. I was shocked by the pictures they were showing me. As on Tuesday, the therapy was followed by another exam, this time Engineering Science. With only me in the subject there was never anyone to talk to about revision, anyway I didn't feel well, so I didn't stay long.

Despite being banned from seeing Stephen, I met him that Friday night in town. We hugged. I told him about the AT, explaining what was going on. He said that he was not getting AT. "Just go with it," he said, "Just try to bluff it out and do what they say."

I told him that I needed him more than ever now, but I knew deep down that our relationship was over. I said that if I wasn't going to see him again after the end of the term, would he please give me something to remember him by.

I should have had my second Engineering Science 'A' level on Tuesday, but I didn't bother going. What was the point? I couldn't get my head sorted out. All I could think about was tomorrow.

### Wed 14th June

I turned up at the hospital for another therapy session. I saw the psychiatrist before the session. The grumpy one who had seen me the first time. He asked me how I was getting on and I just mumbled something like okay. He told me that I would be expected to attend therapy during the summer. As usual, I had never thought ahead much. I had my final 'A' level that afternoon, General Studies, but I never even left the pub. When some of my mates asked me why I hadn't turned up for my exams, I just said I was poorly. I could hardly tell them that I was being treated with electric shocks to cure me of my evil disease.

Despite my hard exterior, I was actually a big softie, and Stephen knew it. After the exams, with the end of the school looming, we met up again. For the last time. He said he had a present for me and he gave me a metal pentagram. The five pointed star was about 3 inches across. He said it was to protect me from evil, meaning the AT. I said "It's made of lead, won't it bend?" to which he said he had made it for me with lead and antimony explaining that antimony was to give greater hardness and strength to the star. He went out of his way to make a pentagram cast, find the metals and melt them down and make my star. I have always kept Stephen's Pentagram close throughout my life.

CHAPTER SIX

# A Shocking Summer

## They must think I am stupid

The aversion therapy continued through the summer holidays. It was initially on Wednesday mornings, but I changed it to Thursday afternoons. I did rugby training on Thursday evenings in Bingley, so I had an excuse to come home late. Having the rugby training straight after the aversion therapy helped as I could run and tackle and use up the anger that I often felt after a visit to the looney bin. I got told off by the coaches a couple of times for being too aggressive in training. I think that's what got me picked to play because I often let it rip, full of raging energy that had to be released.

For eight weeks through the summer I got a job working at TRICO, The Rustless Iron Company. I operated a paint sprayer, spraying enamel paint on drainpipes. I sprayed Stephen's capitals, SCR, on the inside of every pipe I painted. I asked for and received every Thursday afternoon off to go to the hospital, though I didn't tell them why.

After the initial shock of the first few weeks of therapy, I slowly learnt to accept it. I knew what they were trying to do. I had to associate the pain with having sex with men, therefore putting me off them. I could understand that. They must have thought I was thick. They asked me which type of men I like, and I just told them I liked hunky blond blokes. I didn't like them at all as Stephen was thin and had black curly hair. They were giving me electric shocks to stop me wanting to go out with men I wouldn't be seen dead with.

I was an 18-year-old who had a relationship with a 17-year-old, and the occasional sex I had had with young men up to then wasn't half as enjoyable as just walking through town with Stephen. I didn't want to stop loving him and didn't want the electric shocks to deter me from loving him. When they punished me in school, I used to put up with pain, and I'd had enough painful times with visits to dentists. However, whereas in the dentists I could close my eyes, here I couldn't. I tried my best to imagine I was somewhere else but it was hard to do. When I tried to slow my breathing down the sharp pain kept bringing me back.

I think the fact that I didn't get an electric shock when a photo of a woman was displayed was supposed to make me want a woman. It didn't make sense to me because I worked out that if the picture was a woman then the next photo would be a man and I would tense myself for the shock that was coming. Therefore, I was in a tense situation when I saw a woman and in pain when I saw a man. It was like a warning, see a woman, become anxious as the next photo would be a man and I would be shocked.

Was the therapy designed to make me turn to women just because I couldn't go out with men? Were they trying to make me so desperate for sex that I would just have to find a woman. I thought it was more likely to put me off sex completely, which in the end it did.

Even though I sort of got used to it, it was still very distressing, and while sitting in the electric chair the anticipation was both a mental and physical torture. You know you are going to get an electric shock, and while waiting for it to happen, you realise there is not a damn thing you can do to stop it. I would tense my right shoulder all the way up to my neck and wait for the jagged bite into my forearm.

## Back to school

On the 15th August, I received my A-level results. It was as I thought, I'd failed nearly everything. I did get an O level in Chemistry, which is what you get if you are just below the pass mark. That was because I did sit one exam before the AT started. I even failed General Studies, and I think I was the first one in years to have done so. General Studies was just a simple exam put in so that everybody got at least one A level, to justify the education system.

I thought *'Oh dear the shit'll hit the fan now'*, but it never did. It was decided for me by all adults that I should do another year at school. I didn't question it. I never told my parents about the aversion therapy. I didn't tell my brothers about it either. I didn't tell anyone about the AT for many years. I just kept everything hidden away behind a thickened wall.

I returned to school in September 1972 to enable me to try again to pass my exams. It was still possible I could get into university. I dropped engineering science to concentrate on the maths and chemistry. I had more time to study now as Stephen wasn't around anymore.

The AT treatment carried on through the autumn, going once or twice a week. I left school, walked up to the hospital, I did a session and then returned to the school. All very routine. I had to learn to carry on as if nothing had happened. The outer face of the wall that I had built to protect the gay boy was developed to a point where I could almost automatically hide my true feelings within. I couldn't discuss my feelings with any of my friends. I feared rejection if my friends found out.

I was just going through the motions and hopefully telling the priests and doctors what they wanted to hear. I thought I was in control as much as they were. Maybe sooner or later they would call it a day. The priests at school still had me in for weekly talks; they had stopped telling me I was diseased but still encouraged me to keep going with the treatment. I still felt the threat of expulsion from school hanging over me, so I had to continue going to the loony bin.

### Life's not fair

While sitting at home one day I heard the phone ring. I was going to ignore it, but then I heard my mum shout from upstairs,

"Get that will you, Jeremy and if it's Noreen tell her, I'll call her back.

I picked up the phone and said, "Hello."

"Is that you, Jeremy?" I couldn't believe my ears, it was Stephen. I hadn't heard from him since the final day at school last June. I was so relieved to hear his voice.

"Yes, Stephen, it's me. Where are you?"

"I'm at home, do you want to meet up in town?"

"Yeah, I'd love to see you. I've missed you so much. Where've you been?"

"Oh, here and there. I'll tell you all about it when we meet up. By the bus stop as usual?"

"Yeah, I'll get the first train, be there about six. See you soon." As I ran upstairs to change,

Mum said, "Who was it?"

"Just one of my mates, I'm going out."

Sitting on the train all I could think about was Stephen. I imagined kissing and hugging him. My thoughts about him were such that I hadn't noticed it had started snowing. When I came out of the station in Bradford, it was blowing a blizzard. As I crossed the city centre, I lifted the hood of my parka jacket, stuffed my hands deep into my pockets and soldiered on. No snowstorm was going to stop me seeing Stephen. When I arrived at his bus stop, rather than standing out in the snow, I crossed the road to use a bus shelter. His bus arrived, and as it pulled away, I saw him through the snow. He saw me and ran across the road, but to my horror, he slipped on the snow and fell in front of a vehicle going past, which ran him over. Looking down at him, I couldn't move. I wanted to go to him, but I couldn't reach him.

The only person I'd ever loved was lying dead in the road. Looking at him I started to shake and thought I was going to throw up, but I didn't. There was a dark alley at the back of the building behind me. I struggled up it, slipped down into the snow, sat there and cried. I mustn't tell anybody I was here. They had banned me seeing him, and I had broken that rule.

There was only one person to blame for his death, and that was me.

## Living in silent depression

I felt that I had gone through all that pain for the last six months and now I was left with nothing but memories of Stephen. I still felt my love for him. I certainly went nowhere near his house, or funeral or anything. What happened in the days following Stephen's death, I can't remember clearly. It's all a bit blank. I am fairly sure I told someone that Stephen had been killed in a road accident but I can't remember who. I didn't tell them that I had witnessed it. The aversion therapy stopped around this time too.

I kept the whole thing hidden. I couldn't grieve publicly, so I grieved inside. My stomach churned every time I thought of Stephen slipping on the road. Back at school no-one mentioned Stephen. I had learnt from my past experiences not to talk about it, not to show anything, and I didn't for a long time. This was part of my life that no-one else needed to know. All my memories of him were mine to keep and not to be shared with anyone. I didn't tell anyone about seeing Stephen die for nearly ten years.

When I returned to school after the Christmas holidays, I settled down into a sort of depressed silence. My homosexuality wasn't talked about anymore. The priests and teachers just seemed to accept me as I was. I busily rebuilt my internal wall. The wall I created, to keep my feelings hidden, had to be built stronger than ever. I was determined this time not to let anyone in, and, far more importantly, not to let anything out.

I couldn't understand why they didn't expel me. I still thought I was a homosexual. The school staff seemed to be very careful around me after the AT had finished. I got away with events at school for which previously I would have been punished. Swearing at teachers and being short in my answers, maybe they thought I was a bit brittle after the AT and needed to go easy on me.

Typical of my time at school at that time, occurred one day in the school library. We had a gambling card game going, with money on the table, when the Deputy Head came in. I had my back to him so he could not see my face.

"What is going on here?" He demanded, "this is a chess class, not a gambling school."

I'd had enough of teachers by now interfering with what I did and, turning around I said,

"Why don't you just fuck off?" He made a move towards me, and I thought he was going to hit me, then he looked down and recognised me, he stopped, turned on his heels and stormed out of the room slamming the door so hard that all the windows in it shattered.

One of the other boys said, "you're in for it now, Jeremy." I thought I'd be getting another dose of the strap at least, but nothing happened.

One of my maths teachers held me back at the end of class one day and said. "I know what you are going through, Jeremy and if you ever want to talk it about you can come to see me."

"You must be fucking joking, sir; there's no way I'll ever talk to a fucking teacher again." He was visibly stunned by my aggression as I continued, "just bloody well leave me alone."

I endured at school for another six months, taking A-level re-sits but in the end only ever passed one, a D in chemistry. I realised that when the AT had started, my academic life had failed and I found it almost impossible to sit in an exam room and concentrate. The memory of last year's events hung around inside me. I spent a lot of time getting drunk, trying to forget, and, when on my own, crying.

## CHAPTER SEVEN

# Becoming gay

### Jobs and things

When I was looking for my first job after leaving school, my dad told me to work in the textiles industry, "You'll always have a job in textiles," he said. Did that mean he thought that having failed my exams I would be no good as an engineer? I got a job in a dye house at a local firm. It was ok, but I wanted something better. I acquired a position as an assistant to the assistant manager in the Chemical Finishing Department of a large textile mill ten miles from home.

I set myself to my new trade. I worked twelve-hour shifts, keeping myself busy, learning how to work. I found that I liked the practical nature of the job. It was very tactile work, testing the cloth by how it felt between my fingers. My boss, Chris, was a very good teacher. He kept bringing me collections of different cloths, called patterns, to compare with the finished product. I had then to work out how much of each particular chemical would produce the required result when the finished patterns came out of the tentering machines. I could test out my results by knitting all the different patterns together and sending them through the finishing process. I did not need to know the chemical formulas for anything. I just needed to feel the results. Definitely a hands-on job. It became instinctive.

I was sent to college to study Textile Finishing, but failed my first year exams. I just couldn't sit in an exam room and concentrate without remembering the electric shocks. I convinced Chris of my ability to do the job without any academic qualifications.

Even though the mill was only ten miles from home, I had to catch two buses to get there and two back. This made for a very long fourteen hour day. In 1974 I bought a 50 cc motorbike. My bike made it far easier to get to work and also to get away to the mountains to go walking. I spent most of my holidays visiting the mountains of the Lake District, North Wales and Scotland on my own.

There was something about being in the mountains that appealed to me. I felt alive but only if I was on my own. I was happier on my own because I could just relax and be with Stephen. I would cry my eyes out as I remembered how Stephen had died. Then laugh out loud as I remember him singing "Doobedood'ndoobe, Doobedood'ndoobe, Doobedood'ndoo," as he skipped down the corridor towards me.

## Coming out

After my twenty-first birthday, I could go out for sex legally. I spent my evenings going into Bradford or Leeds, going to gay pubs and parties. I had a lot of sex with a lot of men, young and old. A reaction I guess to everyone trying to suppress my sexuality. I didn't have any long term relationships, just one night stands with no love involved. There was one lad my age, I can't remember his name now, who I had a short relationship with, but it never got serious.

In among everything else in my gay life, I'd become a glam rock fan and had taken to wearing bangles. My favourite bands were the Sweet, and David Bowie. I began to appreciate androgynous men. My sex life was only with males. I was at one party when a blond girl came up to me and asked, “Are you a virgin, Jeremy?”

“No,” I said “I have had sex with loads of men. I am gay you know.”

“I mean, have you had sex with a girl?”

“Er ... No, why?”

“I will go to bed with you if you give me your bangles.”

So there was an offer any normal man couldn’t refuse. But I was definitely not a normal man.

“No, sorry, I have no wish to have sex with you or any girl, and anyway, I quite like my bangles,” she smiled at me, “It’s your loss, Jeremy,” and off she went in search of straightening out some other gay lad. I might have gone with her if she’d had black curly hair and looked like Stephen.

I found the whole process of having to act both straight and gay very tiring. I had to develop into two people. At home, I had to act normally. Also at work and out with my straight mates, I acted the same way. I had to be watchful, cautious. Going into the city to visit gay bars, I came more into my own. Then I didn’t have to act. I could just relax and be me.

I found it very hard to make decisions. Endlessly weighing up my options. I was still letting other people make decisions for me. I needed to take charge. On Boxing Day December 1974, I made a very big decision. I waited until my mum and dad were alone in the house and sat on their comfy chairs in the living room. I sat on the settee facing them, my mouth feeling dry and, taking a deep breath, I said, “I have something I have to tell you.” They both looked at me.

“I am a homosexual; I am gay. I like going out with boys, rather than girls.”

My mum's face dropped, and she was silent for a while. By the look in her eyes, I could tell she was shocked and upset. My dad just looked at me, and then with a sneer in his voice he said,

"You are not really gay. It is a shame that such a lovely word has been ruined by associating it with something so disgusting."

"You know what the Bible says about homosexuality don't you?"

I ignored his question and looked at my mum.

"Are you sure?" she said.

"Yes, I am sure, I have been like this for years." I don't think she believed me.

"I'm sure it's just a phase, you'll snap out of it when you meet a nice girl." she said.

"If you choose to live like that you know you are sinful?" said dad.

"It's only sinful to Catholics, Dad, and since I am not a Catholic anymore, it is not sinful for me."

"Well, I think you should be ashamed of yourself. We are not going to talk about this again. I don't want to hear anything more about it." he said, and with that comment, he got up and left the room.

Initially, my mum was quite supportive and told me that she loved me whatever I was. Afterwards, she changed her mind, and she could not accept it. I think my dad had got to work on her. I suppose it was too much of a shock to them, they being so religious. To them, I was a sinner and always would be. At least they didn't tell me I was diseased like the priests at school.

They wouldn't talk about it. They just didn't accept it. They blamed me, blamed themselves, blamed the Devil but never blamed their God. Sex on TV was even more vigilantly avoided. I should have left home, but my dad hardly charged me anything to stay.

Despite my fears, my dad didn't throw me out as I thought he would. I wouldn't have minded if he had, I was making good money and could have found somewhere else to live. It wasn't until I was in my late fifties that I realised the reason he did not throw me out and charged me so little rent was that they wanted to keep their eyes on me. There was one point when I nearly bought a house, but my dad told me that I shouldn't enter such a long-term commitment like a mortgage. He said I wouldn't be able to afford it and anyway I could always live at home cheaper.

Although I was forever thinking of Stephen, I wanted to put my troubled past behind me. I wanted to get more out of gay life than just sex hunting. I decided to get more involved with the fight for gay rights.

I first joined the Campaign for Homosexual Equality (CHE). I felt the CHE were mainly older people campaigning for change quietly but not dynamic enough to actually change anything. So I joined the Gay Liberation Front (GLF) as well. I thought the GLF were a bit more aggressive in their demands for equality. I think it could be said that in the long run, CHE proved more successful than the more anarchic GLF. I helped with fund-raising by organising gay discos. It was such a freedom to be able to dance and sing in the company of like-minded people.

A group of us were gay-bashed on the way home from a gay disco in Bradford. A gang of skinheads were waiting for us outside, and I got a good kicking. Going home covered in bruises was easy to explain away as I just blamed it on playing rugby.

In January 1975 I came out with a vengeance, something I should have done when I was eighteen. It didn't seem like it was only three years before, that I was so frightened of being exposed as queer that I agreed to be cured, but I was a completely different person then. I'd gained a lot of self-confidence from my work with CHE and GLF. I'd grown a thick skin and a devil-may-care attitude. I decided that if I was still diseased, I might as well enjoy it. I found that I could still have friends even though I was a homosexual. I stopped thinking about myself as being queer and became gay.

My best straight friend was Stuart. Now there's a thing, I could have just said my best mate Stuart, but then the reader might have thought he was gay. I have to use the word straight to inform you he was not gay. Stuart was eight years older than me, and one of the most solid friends anyone could have. We often played darts and pool at the Catholic Club in Keighley. I know I had denounced all things Catholic, but the Club was where all my straight mates used to go for the cheap beer. Stuart and I had been beer drinking, dart playing buddies since I joined the Club at eighteen. He managed the Club football team. He coined my nickname of 'Watch your shins Gavins,' which reflected the number of shins I made contact with being late in the tackle while playing for the team.

When I told Stuart I was gay, he accepted me unconditionally. One night as we played darts in the Club, I said to him,

"I am thinking of coming out completely, and I wondered what you thought?"

"You know me, Jeremy, I trust your judgment, you must do whatever you think fit. You know I will always watch your back whatever you do. What are you thinking of?" I told him what I wanted to do, and asked him if he would meet me outside the Club the following night.

"See you at seven." he said, "I think you may shock a lot of people, and I wouldn't miss it for the world."

The following night when we entered the Club, I was wearing my Gay Liberation Front T-shirt festooned with gay badges. Everyone knew me there, but very few knew I was gay. I felt out and proud. Comments ranged from, "Queer bastard," and, "I always thought you were a puff," to "Well done," and, "Gosh, you must be brave." Over the next few months, I was surprised how many members came to talk to me quietly, indicating they were closet gays.

It took a couple of days for my parents to hear about what I had done, and I got a good telling off from my dad. I had embarrassed them, he said. I think my mum had finally got the idea at last, by saying "If you must go in the Catholic club with your Gay T-shirt on, then at least please don't sit under the picture of the Pope."

Coming out at the Club lead to one inevitable result. I experienced another gay bashing. One night a few weeks after I came out, a group of members grabbed me as I left the club and bashed my head against a stone wall in the club car park. Someone called the police. The copper that turned up knew me. He came over and said, "It serves you right for being a queer, Gavins, and if I hear of any revenge, I will be coming to arrest you and not them."

I kept myself busy all the time. I was at work, having sex somewhere, playing rugby, drinking with Stuart or weekends in the mountains. So, with all those activities on the go, staying with my parents, though we didn't get on, suited me very well. It was just a place to sleep, get my washing done and recover my energy or sober up. Whenever I was stuck watching TV with them, I would still get my pack of cards out, play patience and leave my body sitting there. In my mind, I would be off walking the fells or dancing at a disco.

My career was going very well. I worked myself up through the ranks until after only two years I was running the department. Chris had left and recommended me for his replacement. I was a shoo-in. I was a Textile Finishing Technician. Along with an increase in responsibilities I got a good pay rise. I got onto staff pay. This meant I was paid if I had time on sick, which rarely happened, but not for any overtime, of which I did plenty. I was in charge of men, machinery, buying materials and making sure I kept the textile finishing to a very high standard. I was always happy to get involved when chemical deliveries arrived. Wagon drivers would roll fifty-gallon drums of chemicals off the lorry onto wagon tyres, and the trick was to catch them as they bounced, stand them up at an angle and wheel them away on their edge. I'd shoulder fifty-kilogram sacks of urea formaldehyde off lorries and into the warehouse.

I had a short fling in 1975 with one lad my age, Peter, which was nice while it lasted. Peter was the only one I ever took home with me, and we were in bed together when my dad charged in and said there'll be none of that in this house. Nothing was ever said about it again, another case of me not existing as a gay person at home. My relationship with Peter fell apart when I upset him one night by calling him Stephen, and he wanted to know who Stephen was, but I couldn't tell him, so we went our separate ways.

In late 1975 I set off on a four-day backpacking walk around the southern Lake District. I got a train to Windermere intending to walk over to Ravenglass and catch a train home. I felt increasingly poorly as I walked along, being sick a couple of times, but I just thought it would pass. I went off food but carried on drinking beer. On the evening of the second day, I called in for a pint at the Newfield Inn in the Duddon Valley. The barman said to me,

"Have you looked in a mirror lately?"

"Err … No. Why?"

"You should have a look in a mirror. Go in the women's loo, there isn't one in the gents."

I went in the toilet and saw that my eyes were bright yellow. When I returned to the bar, the barman said, "Have you been feeling poorly?" I told him I had. He looked at me again and said "I think you ought to go and see a doctor" then he reached over, picked up my pint, "you don't need this," he said as he poured my pint down the sink.

So, next day, I packed my gear, walked over to Coniston, caught a bus to Windermere and a train home. I went to see my doctor next day and was whizzed off to the hospital with hepatitis A. At the end of July I weighed twelve stone, and on September 18 this had dropped to eight and a half stone and I was still losing weight. I was very poorly. I was on the sick for six months. I had to lie in hospital and not move for days on end, boring as hell. I occasionally escaped on a wheelchair to the smoking room. Not being able to move much, left me at the mercy of the older patients who hogged the TV switch. It was during this stay in hospital that I took on a lifetime hatred to pureed parsnips, Emmerdale Farm, Coronation Street, and ITV in general.

When I finally went back to work, every time I went for a check-up, I asked the doctor,

"Can I start drinking beer again?"

"No, not yet, Jeremy. Your liver is still not functioning correctly."

So every time I saw the doctor, I asked the same question. I'd been off alcohol for nearly a year when at last I heard the reply "Yes, Jeremy, I think you are clear now but don't drink too much."

On my first drinking session, I found that after just half a pint I was already drunk. 'Bloody marvellous' I thought, ‘this’ll save me loads of money.’ However, it soon became clear that the more times I drank beer, the amount I had to drink to get drunk grew steadily.

One night I collapsed in the Catholic club after a heavy drinking session, far too soon after the hepatitis recovery. I ended up staying in hospital for a night. I was a bit violent on the ward, and they fastened me down into a bed, probably for my own protection, but when I woke up, I completely freaked out, screaming for them to release me. I was seen by a psychiatrist who wanted to keep me in, but I wanted out and had to sign a form to get released. There was no way they were going to keep me in there.

## A glimpse of a different life

Something very positive did result from my long sickness. I was on staff pay but spending very little. The money built up nicely and I bought a brand new Suzuki 185cc bike. I used it to get myself farther away giving me more freedom. Losing all that weight made me fitter too. In the summer of 1977, I booked on a walking/climbing week at The National Mountain Sports Centre at Plas y Brenin in Wales. I enjoyed myself immensely; backpacking, scrambling and rock climbing. I noticed that the instructors were having a really good life. They were the same age as me, but I was obsessed with work, making and spending money, having sex and trying to avoid being at home. I thought if I could get a job working outdoors, I would have a happier life. I also met lots of lovely people, who were non-judgmental about my sexuality.

Another thing that happened as a result of being confined to a bed for so long was that I became celibate for a few months. In recovery when I returned to my previous life, I found that sex had become one-night, and sometimes just one-hour or less stands. I was losing interest in going out in search of something I once enjoyed doing. I gave up worrying about how I looked and I slowly became full-time Jerry. He was the hard drinking, rough playing part of myself. Jeremy the gay boy, was not to be trusted. He was forced inside and only allowed out when I was completely alone.

I was always trying to forget what happened to Stephen, to move on, but his death continued to haunt me. I missed him achingly. I still loved him. I thought of him all the time – nice thoughts but always intermingled with his death and how it was my fault. Slowly these thoughts of Stephen came to take over my life, and I gradually lost all interest in sex and gave up around age twenty-five.

Back on the rugby field, after a good ten years, I had accumulated many injuries; broken ribs; torn knee ligaments, dislocated ankle, elbow and shoulder. The rugby club trainer advised me to pack in rugby as he thought it wouldn't do my body any good in the long run. So in midsummer 1978, I found myself in danger of having to spend more time at home unless I found something else to take up my time.

CHAPTER EIGHT

# Discovering what my hands were for

## Jobs

In 1978, I was losing interest in my textile job. It had changed from being mainly practical to more managerial. I was OK if I was working with my hands, but I struggled when I had to sit in an office and concentrate. I often found myself thinking of Stephen and couldn't focus on what I was doing. I had to get out and change my occupation to something more practical, and outdoors preferably.

So I left the mill and got a job in charge of a dye house in another textile mill. I thought the change of scene would do me good. But it wasn't right for me, so after three months I looked for something else. I had an interview for a Forestry Commission post and got the job. Unfortunately they didn't want me to start for three months, so I looked for something else to keep me busy in the meantime. I got a job working as a trackman with British Rail. Based in Keighley, the post involved working weekends and some nights. These career changes meant my pay packets fell from over £10,000 to under £6,000 per year. Every job change I made I took a pay cut, in my search for something, but I didn't know what.

I found myself working in a gang of men. Suddenly I was shovelling stone, swinging a sledgehammer, cutting down trees, mending the railway lines, maintaining the Permanent

Way, that's what they called the railway. A funny gang too, all characters, some weird, some OK and some downright hilarious. I don't think I'd laughed so much in years. This is what I needed, something to make me laugh and keep my mind off other things. I decided to tell the Forestry that I no longer wanted their job.

One of the best parts of my railway job was rebuilding fallen down dry stone walls. Both sides of most of the railway embankments were walled off from the adjoining fields. Before joining British Rail, I hadn't built an actual stone wall, just plenty of the psychological kind. I wasn't given any proper training at it. I just picked it up as I went along. I really took to walling and, when walking the dog on Ilkley Moor, I'd put up walls for fun. On some of my backpacking walks in the Lake District, if I found a wall gap, I'd stop and repair it. I will always remember my first Lakeland wall repair. It was on a footpath through a wood by the side of the A593 Coniston to Ambleside, near Hollin Bank.

There was something about walling that made me feel good. Stones are inert in most peoples' hands, but in mine, they felt alive. I could sort of sense which stone to pick up to fit where I needed it. Despite the work being physically demanding, I found it mentally relaxing. Though I didn't realise it then, my ability to build dry stone walls would become my saviour in years to come.

One thing that really annoyed me working in a gang, were that nearly all conversations ended up in discussions about having sex. Two men in the gang were always asking me about my girlfriends, and bragged about their wives and talked about sex all the time. I just invented stories to keep them happy. They already thought there was something wrong with me because I read the Guardian, instead of the crappy Sun or the Star. I didn't come out on the railway. I thought it was safer to keep Jeremy well hidden behind one of my psychological walls.

In the future when I became a professional stone waller there was one kind of work that I avoided. This was where I had to work in a gang. Working in very small groups or on my own was always going to be my way.

After my experience rock-climbing in Wales, I decided to join a climbing club. I rang the Leeds Outdoor Pursuits Club (LOPC), and in August 1979 I went to the Grove pub in Leeds to meet them. From then on I went climbing on local crags every Wednesday evening and went away with the climbing club every weekend when I wasn't working. All this was a perfect solution to my problem of living with my parents. I know I should have left home when I worked in the mill; when I had earned more money. Now it was too late as my railway pay wasn't high enough to live on my own and pay for my alcohol intake. I was at last back living my life for the moment.

I got on well with the LOPC. It wasn't a tough, hardened rock climbers club; it was just an enlarged group of mates, some of who were 'extreme' climbers, and some of who were just there for a gentle walk and every level in between. They weren't into bragging about what they could do, and anyone would climb with anyone. I was never very good but could climb to Very Severe if I pushed the boat out. The hardest climb I ever did was Forked Lightning Crack, an E2 at Heptonstall in Yorkshire. I felt happier leading at around Severe. I enjoyed climbing on the big mountain crags, on Scafell, Tryfan, and the Cuillins on the isle of Skye. I was climbing in great places and making lots of new friends.

## Suicidal Pre-Tendencies

My emotions swung from side to side. I was in a state of permanent loss. My love for Stephen forever clashing with the pain of his death. I wished I could find the courage to kill myself and I thought about suicide often. I did try once. I heard that if I drank a bottle of whisky and went to sleep in the winter snow, I would not wake up again. I tried this one winter in the Lake District, but it didn't work, I just woke up in my bed with a bad hangover. I assumed I'd woken up in the snow, returned to the accommodation and gone to bed.

Years later, one of my best climbing club mates, Eileen, told me they were worried about me, came to find me, and brought me back. I was too drunk to remember.

When drunk, I often put myself in danger. On one rock-climbing weekend in Borrowdale, I drank so much barley wine at the Scafell Hotel that I couldn't walk. I had to crawl along following the white lines in the middle of the road, and then, when I got to my tent, I tripped over the guy lines flattening it, and fell asleep on top of it. When I woke up in the morning, I had completely forgotten that it was me that had collapsed my tent and spent all day muttering about campsite vandals.

After climbing at Crag Lough in Northumberland, I did another white line road crawl along the B6318, dodging the traffic after leaving the pub blind drunk. I fractured my left wrist palming off a car in Keighley. I lived a sort of dual lifestyle, veering between sober depression and drunken, suicidal stupidity.

In 1982 during a visit to see Eileen, I was smoking pot and drinking heavily, always a bad combination for me. I couldn't hold it in any longer and told her all about Stephen and how I saw him die. This was the first person I talked to about Stephen and was relieved that she listened, and didn't tell me I was horrible. I told a couple more people in the climbing club too. I needed to release the stress pressure somehow. I could, at last, be more open about my weird behaviour when I would often hide away when drunk and be in tears.

With others, I kept everything so well hidden that one of my rock climbing partners from those days didn't find out I was gay until 2012 and was surprised when I told him. I hadn't told him because I thought he was homophobic. I enjoyed his company as a rock climber, and I didn't want to do anything to spoil that. I'd hidden Jeremy behind my inner wall so successfully that he never knew or guessed. It was probably a good thing I did keep quiet about it because, after I told him, we never met up again.

I often drank huge quantities of beer, barley wines and whisky on these rock climbing weekends. Many years later when I saw Eileen again for the first time in ages, she said that all the climbing club members were amazed that I was still alive, such were my suicidal stupidities when drunk.

CHAPTER NINE

# Rutting

If you walk the fells, you'll often come across dung beetles. Black beasties up to two cm long that trundle around doing their thing with poo. They lumber about looking as if they may overturn at any moment. My life was like that of one of those beetles crossing a deeply rutted field. Slightly different, though, as dung beetles roll up their dung, I just fell head first into it. When in good spirits I'd be happily walking on the top of a rut, then something would happen, tripping me into falling down flat on my face into the mire at the bottom of the next rut. Then, a bit more successfully than that snail of my childhood maths class, I would crawl through the deeply depressing mud before reaching the next wall to climb. 1983 turned out to be a field of deep ruts with narrow tops.

On 12th February 1983, I had the perfect opportunity to kill myself. I twisted my left knee ice climbing. There were three of us, Jim, Dave and myself. We were above Low Water on Coniston Old Man in the Lake District. The snow conditions were perfect for winter climbing. As we made our way up the snow and ice covered crag progress was good. Jim went first, then me, then Dave. We were not tied together with ropes as we thought we wouldn't need to be. But Jim, being the leader, carried one just in case.

I was climbing with two ice axes and crampons. Making my way up I placed my left foot onto what I thought was good ice, but as I put all my weight on my left leg, the ice broke, the crampon caught on a jagged rock, and I felt an excruciating pain in my knee. I lowered myself back down to look at my leg; it was in a horribly twisted out to the left position from my knee downwards. It made me feel quite sick looking at it. I hung on with my right foot and two ice axes and stuck my left leg in a crack and tried to straighten it. Screaming with pain and swearing loudly, I managed to straighten it, but when I tried to stand on it, it locked up again this time at a right angle. Despite the pain I had at least got it into a position I could use it to kneel on.

All I had to do at this point to kill myself was to let go of my axes, but I clung on to them tightly and, despite the pain, I was determined not to fall. Dave came up to find out what was causing all the swearing.

"What's all the fucking noise?" he said, then he saw my twisted leg, "Oh hell, what have you done?"

"I think I've broken my leg." Dave called up to Jim to lower the rope down, and he tied me on. Dave then went down the mountain to call out the mountain rescue team. Jim made me climb up to him and slowly, bit by bit, he got me to climb to the top of the crag. I climbed on one good leg and one knee, with much swearing, and cries of pain.

When I got to the ridge, I was exhausted. All I wanted to do was to lie down and go to sleep in the snow. Jim was having none of that and pushed, prodded and dragged me along to the top of the Old Man. Here we met the rescue team coming up to get me. After assessing my knee problem, they gave me some laughing gas, so from being in pain, I was now all chuckle-some. I needed to be because they couldn't strap me into the stretcher with my knee sticking out, so one of them pulled my leg straight. My scream was so loud it caused avalanches all round the Lakes. Then they made that wonderful move where one rescuer holds the stretcher, and we were both lowered down the crag. On reaching the good track by the tarn, they carried me on the stretcher down to a waiting Mountain Rescue Land Rover which took me down into Coniston. Fifteen years later I would be driving my own Land Rover up this very track as I made my way up the mountain to carry out footpath repair work on the path that I had been carried down.

In hospital, they told me I had torn my knee cartilage, and it would have to come out. I went into hospital on the 1st March, and the next day they took it out. When I woke up after the op, I was thoroughly confused. I couldn't work out where I was, and my whole body started shaking uncontrollably. After they had calmed me down the nurses just said not to worry, it was just the anaesthetic wearing off.

When the doctor made his rounds the next morning, he stopped next to me.

"I thought you might like this as a souvenir of your ice climb," he said, handing me a little bottle of liquid with two pieces of what looked like gristle in it.

"I have never seen anyone tear their knee cartilage in half before. These are both halves of your cartilage Jeremy, in formalin." I've still got it somewhere. Then started a regime of physiotherapy three times a week for the next thirteen weeks.

When I got back on two legs, my doctor recommended walking through deep heather to strengthen my left knee. I spent many days walking on the heather clad hills behind Bolton Abbey, Simon's Seat and the lovely named Valley of Desolation. Walking head held high and fit again I should have known it wouldn't be long before I fell headlong into the next rut.

I started work again on Monday the 6th June and the next day was off again after having been stung by a bunch of wasps while building a dry stone wall alongside the railway tracks. I had used up all my sickness allowance and had to take a week's holiday leave.

Then two weeks later my Suzuki 250cc motorbike got pinched. Two days later, it was found in a canal, a write-off. I was desolate about losing my bike. I'd passed my driving test on it; it reminded me of good looking curly black haired men. It had a silver fibreglass body with "Silver Dream Racer" written down both sides.

Silver Dream Racer was a 1980 motor-racing film starring British pop star David Essex. I'd always fancied David. David was my first dream lover with his black curly hair, long before Stephen imprinted his face over every single boy I had seen up till then. He brought out a song 'The Time of My Life' in 1970 coinciding nicely with my relationship with Stephen. When I saw the bike in the shop, I bought it immediately, trading in my 185cc Suzuki, as part exchange.

Worse was to follow because the government in their whimsy had just changed the law on how many ccs were allowed before a rider had to pass their driving test. It had been 250cc, but it was lowered to 125, so learners lost the right to ride their 250's. This resulted in a rapid decline in the value of a 250cc motorcycle and with it the value of my fully comprehensive insurance. I had paid £850 for my Dream Racer but only got paid £250.00. Typical.

Whenever our railway gang foreman, George, was off sick or on holiday, the sub ganger took charge. In 1983 our old subbie retired, and we acquired a new one. This new one was only twenty-two and a complete nutcase. If he didn't like someone he would pick fights with them just to prove his superiority. In July '83 the crackpot attacked me. I'd had enough of him, and I complained to our boss, who told me to put it in writing, which I did.

I had to go to the Head Office in Leeds to see the personnel manager with the result that the sub-ganger was moved back to his hometown to work, just seven miles up the track. On 13 October 83, we were working at the nutter's home station when I met my nemesis again, and he went for me, this time with a lump of wood, but this time I was backed up by other members of our gang. The guy was manic.

Later I found my new motorbike, a Suzuki GS 550, had been vandalised. I couldn't believe it, what was it with me and motorbikes? Luckily it had just been kicked over, so it was just a paint job and new mirrors. But that wasn't the point; I had an idea who had done it.

When I saw manic-man again, I accused him of it, and we ended up having a fight, I think I lost. Unfortunately, it took place near a station platform, so we were reported by the Stationmaster. For this, we both had to go to York for disciplinary procedures. I thought I was going to get the sack.

At the York meeting on the 9th November, I fought my corner, and George spoke up for me. I kept my job, but the subbie got sacked. Then to cap off the year, on 3rd December 83, playing five aside football in a gym, I dislocated my left elbow and strained my right knee, but on the good side, I received another dose of laughing gas. I could get addicted to this stuff.

To say 1983 was a bad year would be spot on, spending in all twenty weeks on sick leave, having my motorbikes pinched or vandalised, having fights at work and nearly getting sacked. My life as a railway worker was now getting too much. I did think of leaving but in 1984 George retired, and the new ganger was a good man and everything calmed down and turned peaceful again. Just how bad 1983 was, I wouldn't find out for another twenty-eight years.

### Out of my rut

In 1984 I started to cross the bottom of my rut, slowly recovering from my latest injury, still on sick, drinking lots of beer and depressed. I tried to take control of my life again by cutting down on my smoking from thirty a day to ten and getting some walking done. When I got back to work, my arm was good again, I suddenly emerged from my rut, to find myself standing at the edge of a wide flat unrutted field.

I took a training course for the railway job, and I passed a few railway engineering skills, for which I got promoted to skilled trackman and back pay of £699.00! I had to do a lot of track patrolling, walking the track checking for faults.

Patrolling for me was like being paid for doing something I would have done for nothing. Depending on the time of year there were always plenty of raspberries, strawberries, plums, apples, pears and mushrooms to be collected. While walling at this time, I felt I needed to expand my walling experience so sought out training courses and discovered the British Trust for Conservation Volunteers, BTCV. This charity ran practical conservation training courses all over the country. I attended a dry stone walling course in Derbyshire.

Each section of the railway track around the country was graded according to how important it was. The higher the grading, the more the track was patrolled. Our piece was downgraded to just a one day a week patrol. The ganger took over this patrol which meant me going back to working with the gang five days a week. I had got used to doing my own thing as a track patrolman. I didn't want to go back. It was time for a job change.

As I was toying with what I could do, my climbing mate Eileen, suggesting I go to university to study for a degree. As a mature student with five O-levels, she thought I would get in somewhere. I looked around at courses that might interest me. With my best subject being maths, I thought teaching made sense at the time. In December I went to Bradford College for an interview to do a B.Ed. Primary teaching degree course, specialising in mathematics. I got confirmation of acceptance at college on 17th January 1985, to start the following September.

My last day on the railway was 6th September 1985. Throughout this period from 1978, I didn't have sex with anyone. I didn't seek it and nor did I miss it. I had returned to the closet and closed the door behind me.

My obsession with Stephen had a silver lining. He saved me from catching Aids. Without him to love and cherish, I may have kept up my life of endless sexual encounters. Loving Stephen saved my life.

## CHAPTER TEN

# Tests, pass the real ones, ignore the rest

I began my mature student life at Bradford College on 16th September 1985. I started off on a two-year Diploma of Higher Education leading on to a further two year Bachelor of Primary Education. I was not exactly sure why I chose teaching. Did I want to be a teacher? Not sure. Looking back it was a stupid thing to do; I wasn't fit or able to become a teacher.

It wasn't a complete failure. What I did get from college was a huge boost in my self-confidence. The change of career that came about as a result of becoming a student was something I believe would not have happened in any other way.

I still lived at home right up to the age of thirty-two. You may ask why I didn't leave any earlier, as I didn't get on with my parents. I didn't need to. Physically all my brothers left home before me, but I left home sooner than they did when I learnt to leave my body at home as my mind wandered off to find freedom elsewhere.

I was hardly ever there in body either, forever away rock climbing, working or walking. I still considered home somewhere to eat, kip, sober up and get my washing done. But in the second year of college, I finally got away and went to live in a student house in Bradford. Living as a student after being reasonably well paid for the previous twelve years didn't come as such a shock as I thought it would. My grant worked out to be worth about the same per week as a weeks basic pay on the railway. I spent some of my spare time building dry stone walls for local farmers to augment my grant.

I was invited up to a farm on Ilkley Moor to see about some walling. When I drove my bike up to the farm, I had to sit astride my shovel and a five-foot long crowbar, with my pick and sledgehammer sticking up out of my rucksack.

When I got there, the farm seemed deserted. I shouted, "Anybody here?"

"Over 'ere," I heard a shout coming from the barn. I entered the barn and saw a tall chap standing on some scaffolding struggling with a stone lintel. I think he was trying to lift it into a hole in the barn wall. Without him saying anything, I climbed the ladder onto the scaffold. He looked at me and said,

"Get your end on first, then work yoursen towards me and we'll soon 'ave bugger in place." Nothing else was said until the stone was in position. At the bottom of the ladder, he turned to me and said,

"You Jerry?"

"Yes," I said.

"Name's Jeff. Come to do some walling 'ave yeh?"

"Yes."

"The walls are down 'ere," and he set off through a gate and across a field with me jogging along to keep up with him. He stopped next to a fallen down wall.

"Start 'ere an' work yeh way across t' slope until yeh get t' far end."

"You on the dole?"

"Yes."

"I'll pay you £1 an hour." Then he left me to it. I built four yards of wall a day in two ten hour days earning myself £20. Not a lot but, "Owts better than nowt" as Jeff said.

On my third visit I was working away, head down digging out stone, when I heard someone say "Are you claiming unemployment benefit?" Startled, I looked up to see a man in a suit and tie looking over the wall at me. *Ergh*, I thought someone must have reported me, and I was wondering what to do when Jeff stuck his head over the wall laughing "Ha, ha, got you there Jerry, this is my brother, Jim. 'E's a farmer too."

"Bastards," I said, then Jeff said, "I like your walling, Jerry, so I'll pay you the same as my brother pays 'is waller, £5 a yard." Quickly totting that up in my head meant I had earned £40 instead of twenty so far.

"Cheers Jeff, I'll be around with a bill at the end of the week." As they walked away, Jim turned to me and said, "You passed the test then?"

"Eh, what test?" I answered.

"The one where Jeff is up on the scaffold struggling with his pet lintel."

Apparently, Jeff always used the lintel and scaffold trick to test anyone who came to work for him the first time. The fact that I had helped him without being asked meant I was a worthy man. I wonder if he would still think that if he knew I was gay.

I put the long summer holiday of 1986 to great use. I went on a few one week long dry stone walling projects with the BTCV in Derbyshire and Lancashire. I'd toyed with the idea of becoming a professional dry stone waller since 1984 but didn't have the confidence at that time to go it alone, but now I was getting rather good at it and making money too. On one BTCV working holiday in Derbyshire, the leader, who was a professional waller, told me I was good enough to go professional.

In my second year at college, I specialised in maths dropping some of my other subjects. A problem I didn't foresee were the difficulties I would have in the study of Psychology. Freud and co were okay, but when it came to studying behaviourist theories, I realised that these were the ones followed by the psychiatrist in the mental hospital. I felt very emotional about this and disputed the theories with the tutors, but I couldn't tell them why. I had to sit there squirming in my seat during lectures about Skinner. I couldn't get anywhere with that side of psychology. It was made worse when at the end of year exams there was a question about it. When I read the question, I ended up stressing myself when I should have just ignored it and moved on. I failed that part of my course.

Into 1987 and I was back in my rutted field with my mood swings continuing to go up and down, a mix of being positive one day and negative the next. When I moved to Bradford, I got away from the Catholic GP in Keighley. The first time I visited my new GP I told her I was depressed but not about why and said I had trouble sleeping and could she give me some sleeping pills, but she wouldn't. I must have been an obvious suicide risk. She just advised me to take up meditation and go for long walks.

College work continued in fits and starts as the term led inexorably towards my first full-time teaching practice. My pre-visit to the school, on 12th February, was a disaster. As I walked down the corridor to the Headmaster's office, I came across two boys sat at a table doing maths. I asked the Head about them. "They are being disciplined." He said. I asked, "How am I supposed to teach these children maths when you use it as a form of punishment?"

"Don't question my practices, you are only a student." was the reply. I thought this was a bit over the top as I reckon I was probably a couple of years older than him. I came back to college totally disillusioned and told my tutor that I wanted to pack it all in, but he convinced me to carry on after all the work I had put in.

On the 2nd March, I began my five-week Teaching Placement. The first day went OK but not organised enough, 2nd day OK too, and also Wednesday and Thursday, but then came Friday. I lost all control over both my classes and ended up nearly swearing at the kids. I just fell apart. All weekend I agonised over what to do. On Monday morning I went and told my tutor that I was packing in the TP and no longer wanted to do the B.Ed. either.

I must say that having made the decision to quit, I felt mightily relieved. The next day at college I was informed that if I walk off the course now, I would lose (and have to pay back) my grant. My tutor said I should continue with the course but do another form of placement, somewhere other than a school. I went to see the Placements tutor who asked me what I wanted to do. I said it had to be something that involved outdoor work.

He got out his book of placements and what happened next would be the first in a line of positive events which would change my life continuously for the better over the next three years. As the tutor started going through the book in alphabetical order, he got to City Farms. "Will that do?" he asked, I said fine, so he rang them, but no-one answered. I am glad they didn't because the next in alphabetical order were the Conservation volunteers, BTCV. When he rang them whoever answered the phone said of course I could have a placement with them. I didn't tell the tutor that I had been working with the BTCV for the last couple of years. I would have to do an assignment and write up a placement report about the organisation but knew that wouldn't be a problem. So I ended up on a four-week placement going out walling, hedge laying, fencing and tree planting when the week before I was stressing myself out stuck in a school. Life was on the up.

During the Easter holidays, I went on another dry stone walling week in the Lake District at Hartsop in the Ullswater valley. I built some lovely walls, so well that the task leader, Roger, asked me if I was interested in something called the Ullswater Project, a three-month long residential starting the following June, doing practical conservation work around Ullswater Lake. I had impressed him with my walling, and he said he could do with another proven good waller to help him on the project that he would be leading. It would mean going on a selection weekend, but I might get on. I had to think about this. Although it would involve living in the Lakes for three months which would be fantastic, it would also mean I would have to leave Bradford. All my friends were in Bradford, and I was not sure I wanted to go through the depressions I knew would come from moving to live in a new place with no-one I knew. But on 15th April when I received my invitation to attend the Ullswater Project selection weekend on the 24th I accepted straight away.

So, on the 24th I drove my motorbike up to Staveley-in-Cartmel for the Ullswater Project selection weekend. I met the leaders, Roger, Joe, Dave and Charlotte, plus lots of other people. I had trouble sleeping that first night and got up early and went for a walk. As luck would have it, I came upon a fallen down wall. I spent an hour putting it up. There was something about dry stone walling which always settled my mind. Saturday was happily spent felling pine trees on a local nature reserve, followed by pub in the evening. On Sunday we went over to Ullswater to look at some worksites.

The selection process was more or less a personality group test to see how people got on with each other both working and socially. I managed to stay positive and got involved in everything. I wrote in my diary 'Oh please, please let me be accepted.' I had set my mind on being chosen and didn't know what I would have done had I not been. I got a letter confirming my place, 'Yes, I've passed the test,' it says in my diary. All I had to do now was to contain myself until it started. I thought a whole change of scene and something so different would brighten up my life's depressions. I knew that doing hard physical work was something I enjoyed and I was looking forward to building dry stone walls in the Lake District.

My life as an academic student was gladly coming to an end, and my life as a practical conservation worker was developing. I was doing some very good walling at this time, both voluntary for the BTCV and for farmers. I realised that I was probably good enough to make it as a professional dry stone waller. I would use the Ullswater project to improve my skills and hopefully become a Lake District waller.

But, as usual, whenever I start feeling too good about things, something rotten happens. On 31st May, someone pinched my GS 550 Suzuki motorbike from outside my house in Bradford. I reported it to the police, but I never saw it again. Without my motorbike I was very restricted on my travels, I couldn't afford another. The insurance people said it would take eight weeks to pay out.

CHAPTER ELEVEN

# The Spaceship

On 10th June 1987 at age 33, I finally lost my virginity to women. I went to bed with one of my fellow students, we were just two lost souls seeking comfort, but as much as anything else this proved to me that I wasn't interested in women's bits, their minds I loved, but their bodies were not for me.

The Ullswater Project started on the 13th June. The centre was at Greenside Mines in Glenridding. I arrived mid-afternoon, and by late evening almost everyone had turned up. Luckily for me, the ones that I'd got on with the best from the selection weekend had been chosen.

For income, we all had to sign on the dole in Penrith. Having been unemployed in Bradford, where the queue to sign on used to go out into the street and around the corner, the size of the dole office in Penrith amused me. It was so small that only about half a dozen people could fit in and the only person I saw sign-on was a gentleman in a very smart suit.

The next three months went like a breeze with added mud and rain, getting stuck into lots of practical work, getting on with some people, average with others and I only fell out with one man. There were a fair number of drinking sessions. It's a wonder where we found the money but needs must. Most of the group were around twenty-one-year-old graduates, just out of college or university.

I spent most of my leisure time with half the group, mainly women, and avoided all the macho young men. One woman, in particular, an ex-nurse Alison, was the best. One specific thing I have got to thank Alison for is the fun of writing letters to people. At the centre, when the post arrived, there was always lots for Alison and not much for anyone else. When I asked her why she always got post, she said, "Do you write to anyone?" When I said "No," she laughed and said, "How can you expect anyone to write to you if you do not write to anyone else?" In the next century when everyone was busy keeping in touch via the internet I would still be writing letters to my friends on paper.

There was something about practical work that, although physically demanding, I found mentally beneficial in that when I got stuck into something I never thought about the past. Despite that, I always found the pain returned when the work stopped. With my sleeping disturbed, I slowly felt the pressure building up within myself again. There didn't seem to be any way out of these negative thoughts; in Bradford, I had managed to find the courage to tell some people about Stephen, but up here no one knew, and with no one to talk to, I was stressing myself out again.

I was working hard, cutting down on beer, tiring myself out physically but still, I couldn't sleep, and when I eventually did, I had a nightmare about being on a bloody spaceship.

> *I am on a spaceship flying through space light years from nowhere in particular, travelling I know not where. I am strapped in my seat watching, looking out of a window. I am in control. I dock with another spaceship to refresh supplies and meet some people, and then it's*

*off again somewhere else. Then I sense a presence on the ship, something horrible, and I leave my cockpit and go into the ship. Suddenly I feel that I am losing control and must escape. I spend a lot of time trying to find somewhere to hide. Trying to be quiet because there is something searching for me, some kind of relentless robot. There is a secret key to a place where I will be safe, but I can't find it. I creep around the ship looking for the key when I meet a small boy who shows me a place where I will be safe. I enter the place and feel safe. But after a while, I begin to get afraid in the dark, and I turn on a light to see where I am. I start to search for the boy again, but all I do is reveal myself to the robot searching me out. I quickly try to hide but it corners me, and I know it's going to kill me. I try to make peace with this thing but can't, so I make one more attempt to escape. I get back into the cockpit of my spaceship, and just as it gets hold of me, I look out of the window and see that the spaceship is about to collide with an asteroid and realise that I have lost all control. If only I could have stayed in control, I would have been safe, and then I feel the crash and the metal shooting through my body before I black out. When I wake, I am shaking and trembling uncontrollably.*

I thought I was a very strange gay man. I didn't have any relationships with men and liked the company of women. It has always confused me this friendship I had with certain women. I definitely felt gay, but I like the company of women. I didn't have to pretend to be macho and liked them as people, not as sex objects which is what most men talked of. It was a good way of hiding my sexuality too.

Roger, the group leader, lent me a book, "The Little Prince" by Antoine de Saint-Exupery. In it, I found the lines:

"To forget a friend is sad, not everyone has had a friend," and

"It is such a secret place, the land of tears."

These two lines made me feel both sad and happy at the same time. Happy that I had a friend in Stephen and sad that I had lost him. I know it would have been good for me to have a relationship with someone but throughout my thoughts every day was my love for Stephen. I yearned for him every day, which reminded me of his death and my fault. There was no room in my life for anyone else. I thought these feelings would subside in their strength, but they never did.

Finally, on a lovely walk in the Langdales, I told Alison and Jo I was gay and then later couldn't stop thinking it was a mistake. I liked Alison and feared how she would react to me now, I hoped I hadn't lost her friendship by telling her I was gay, but she was fine with it. At last I could relax with some of them and take some stress off myself, and as usual, they were okay with it. Why oh why do I always have a huge fear of talking about my sexuality? I felt that at least if they know a little about me, they might forgive me when I get down about things.

On the fifth of August, I had a terrible night's sleep. I had a nightmare where I was trying to escape something, but I didn't know what. I woke up as some of the volunteers pulled me back from climbing out of a window, saving me from a ten-foot drop. I was getting anxious now that despite my opening up to people, working physically very hard, and feeling better; I was getting weird nightmares that were getting worse.

Behind the centre, the fell rose up steeply to Sheffield Pike. Whenever I wanted to be alone, I went up there for a walk. On the fellside, I found a large slab of rock that was just the right size and angle to lie down on and look up at the sky. On one particularly night lying on my rock, I watched an incredible moonrise over the fells. The moon knows all my secrets; it is just like me, pitted and cratered from its past, with half of its body forever hidden from view.

I often felt those loving emotions I felt when I was with Stephen. I wanted to take these positive feelings and build on them. But then I am always doing this and never getting anywhere and knew that it was only a matter of time before I dropped once more into despair.

(I didn't know it then, but it would be a good eleven years before the full strength of my depressions came back).

In August I got a £750 insurance pay out for my stolen motorbike. I immediately invested half on a 'Learn to Drive a car in a Week' course which would take place when the Ullswater Project had ended.

Just before the project finished in mid-September, Roger bought me a book for my birthday, Jonathan Livingston Seagull by Richard Bach. This book became my bible. It went a long way towards improving the way I thought about my life. I should do my own thing. Because of the way I have started to live my life, I ought to live as myself, and not be scared of how other people see me. I wasn't to know it at that time, but it would take over thirty years to find that freedom.

Along with another three of the Project volunteers, I decided to continue doing voluntary work with the BTCV in the Lake District. I found somewhere to live in Windermere, a winter let from October onwards.

Having no particular place to go, and no means of getting there, I camped up in the Lakes for a couple of weeks. Then I returned to Bradford to do my driving lessons. The course was supposed to get me up to pass standard in one week. I drove for six hours every day for five days and then took the test at the end of it. The driving was fantastic, driving all around Yorkshire and I got up to speed well.

On the day of the test, I happened to hesitate at one junction, was honked at and overtaken. Then a thunderstorm decided to test me, and I was found wanting. I drove far too slowly around the backstreets of Bradford and failed. I was way before my time though because all those back streets now have a twenty mph speed limit and speed bumps on them. Anyone doing the test there now can pass going as slow as I did. Included in the contract for the driving course was a statement that if I failed my test the next one would be free. I then bummed around Keighley and Bradford until the end of October when I moved back to the Lakes to the rented house in Bowness.

Like other times in my life, when I changed direction career-wise, I threw myself into my new job as a voluntary field officer for the BTCV. Working outdoors, in all weathers, learning all sorts of new countryside skills, meeting lots of people, making new friends. The Field Officer, Charlotte, was a bit hesitant at the beginning to figure out what to do with us all but as we were all pretty clued-up regarding practical work she just let us get on with it. We divided out responsibilities with me taking on midweek leadership and looking after all the tools and materials. The tools job was perfect for me because, if I ever wanted to be alone, I could escape to the tool store and mend tools, sharpen things and keep my mind occupied.

Charlotte came into the tools store one day, and she brushed her thumb across one of the billhooks to see how sharp it was, cutting her thumb. I don't think she had ever had her tools so well looked after and sharp.

My life was just one long working holiday, walling and walking in the mountains and rock climbing too. There was not much time for me think too deeply and slowly I began to get over my past. It's not that I forgot about Stephen, it was just that yet again I managed to force these thoughts back behind my inner stonewall.

In December I returned to Hollybush Farm in Leeds for a Working Holiday Leadership Training course. Leaders were responsible for everything; shopping, cooking, health and safety, training and entertainments officer. Over New Year 1987/8, I lead my first working holiday, coppicing at Whitbarrow in South Lakeland. Coppicing is a form of woodland management which involves cutting down small trees, mainly hazel, allowing light onto the woodland floor encouraging new growth. With new growth come more insects which bring in the birds, and everything lives, eats each other and dies, in harmony.

On 6th Jan, '88 I passed my driving test in Kendal. I told the examiner I could kiss him for passing me. He declined my offer. Now I needed a vehicle. I'd opened an account with Barclays Bank when I moved up to the Lakes, and I went to ask them for a bank loan. They were hesitant at first because I was on the dole. I told them it was to buy a vehicle which would help me get a job, so they lent me £1000. I bought an Escort van for £750. Stuart, my mate from Keighley, being a mechanic, came to check it over. Between the two of us, he made sure it was a good buy for me, and I made sure it was a goodbye for me too, by allowing me to say goodbye to cadging lifts off everyone.

In mid-January, I had another downer. I don't know what brought it on, but I got terrible headaches with lots of shaking, and I retreated behind my inner stonewall. Following my Bradford GP's advice, I went out for a long meditative walk up the Langdales where the wind blew my bad thoughts away. Charlotte asked me if I was all right, if I wanted to talk. I told her that I was gay, but that it was not being gay that got me depressed but Stephen's death. She was okay with it, and I think we became good mates. She started referring to me as her Dour Yorkshireman. The first word could be pronounced as Do-er or Dow-ur depending on what mood I was in at the time. I think she noticed that I was never dour when I was doing something practical.

Around mid-March, the Windermere dole office began to get on my back about getting a job. I would have stayed doing voluntary conservation work forever if I could. I started looking for jobs in a similar vein. I had an interview for a National Trust Estate workers job but was unsuccessful. I thought I would like to continue as a volunteer but in a different part of the country.

CHAPTER TWELVE

# A Scottish Adventure

On 2nd April, I rang Scottish Conservation Projects on the off chance that they might want me. SCP was the BTCV equivalent in Scotland. After explaining my wishes, Keith, the Field Officer, who answered the phone said:

"You might be interested in the jobs we have just advertised." These were for three Seasonal Field Assistants, which were low paid working holiday leaders. I jumped at the chance of an interview and drove up to Doune, near Stirling, the next day. At the end of the interview, I got offered one of the posts, to start on 9th April.

It reminded me of March 1987 . . . when City Farms didn't answer a call that lead me directly to the Conservation Volunteers. I just happened to ring at the right time. Maybe someone was looking after me. I thought it might be Stephen, but why now, when he had died so long ago?

So I said my farewell to the Lakes for a while and set off to Scotland. The Scottish working holidays were similar to the English ones apart from the fact that they were mostly for ten days and sometimes longer. I reported for work at the base in Doune. During a busy first week, SCP provided me with a twelve seater Land Rover Station Wagon, a horsebox trailer that had to be packed to the gunnels with equipment, cooking gear and everything to make me self-sufficient, apart from food, for a couple of months. All the tools I would foreseeably need were carried in the coffin. This was an eight-foot-long metal box which lived on the roof-rack. At the start of each project the coffin had to be completely emptied and at the end filled up again in a sequence which, if not followed correctly, would mean the tools wouldn't all go in, then it would have to be emptied and started again. It became my least favourite job which, unfortunately, I couldn't delegate to anyone else.

I loved the freedom I was given to sort out what was needed and took advice from the other leaders about items I would probably need which hadn't occurred to me. There would be no facility for nipping back to the depot for anything missing, as all the sites were far away in the north of Scotland. I could draw on the experience I had from doing my conservation work and organising workforces in the mill and on the railways.

Then, with my first list of volunteers to pick up along the way, I set off to Old Deer, to the west of Aberdeen for my first project. There were only two volunteers, Wendy and Angela, but what we lost in numbers we made up with in sheer involvement, organisation and lots of hard work. The work was a bit odd in that it involved digging out all the turf from within the ruins of the buildings of Deer Abbey and replacing it with gravel, so visitors could work out where the insides and the outsides of the buildings of the old Abbey were. I had to learn to drive a two-ton dumper to help our little team shift all the many tonnes of soil and gravel back and forth across the site. My long summer of contentment had got off to a good start. Both Wendy and Angela had been on previous Scottish projects so knew what needed doing when.

My schedule took me from Deer Abbey to the Black Isle, east of Inverness, building bridges in the Fairy Glen, near

Rosemarkie. An example of my new found self-confidence, came as we were building bridges in the Glen. We had to carry a pair of twenty-seven feet long logs up a winding path to the site. There were only six of us; we couldn't even lift one off the ground never mind carry them. So I went around all the pubs in the area and asked if I could have some big strong lads as volunteers to help us next day, a Saturday. When we got to the site, there were seventeen of them waiting for us. One of the lads asked if they could caber toss them and I told him I didn't care how they got them to the site so long as they didn't break them. I didn't even need to carry them; I just pointed out where we wanted them, and they all got stuck in, and the job was done in less than an hour.

After playing in the fairy glen, my next project was at a fairy castle, Brodie Castle near Nairn, for a very muddy dry stone walling task. Whoever had done the site visit had failed to spot the field drain that passed under the wall. We had a JCB digging out the base of the wall. When it hit the drain, the site was flooded. The water eventually drained away; the mud didn't.

For my next project, I drove across Scotland from one coast to the other for a month of mortar walling at Armadale Castle on Skye. I found it exciting when I had to pick up new volunteers at the start of each project. Some volunteers did a couple of the tasks at a time, so I had sometimes help with my chores. I don't think I had time for any negativities to find their way into my thoughts. One thing that definitely cut down on my depressions was that, though I wasn't teetotal, my beer drinking was cut down to a very low level due to all the driving I had to do.

All these projects involved me doing the training and supervision for the practical work. On jobs I hadn't done before I took instructions from the BTCV Practical Conservation work handbooks for whatever project we were on. It was a great learning experience. I found that I could turn my hand to any practical conservation job, and sometimes improve on it, just by doing it once.

After the first two months of tasks, I had a one week break and, after a few days in Yorkshire, it was back to Doune for the next two months. I started off bridge building at the Birks of Aberfeldy, then I had two days to drive all the way to the top end of Scotland to Thurso to catch a ferry to the Orkneys. Here I stayed for twenty-seven days. I loved being left alone to drive around Scotland.

On the island of Hoy, we erected post and wire fencing across peat bogs. I impressed the volunteers with my bird knowledge when driving to the worksite one morning on Hoy. I saw a bird flying straight towards us, and I said "Look there's a short-eared owl" I stopped the Landrover and they all jumped out to watch it, amazed at my eyesight. Actually, I had just read a little leaflet about birds on Hoy and guessed. It could have been a sparrow for all I know about birds, of any kind.

Then it was off to Rousay for ten days of dry stone walling on the beach. A fantastic site. This was the first time I'd ever had the pleasure of building a dry stone wall so close to the sea. The stone for the wall came straight off the beach. You'd think that it would be impossible to build such a good wall with water washed boulders, but the stone here was just flattish with only curved ends. The volunteers found the stone perfect for skimming into the sea which, though it didn't help the wall building, at least gave those who were no good at walling some form of pleasure.

That was it for the Orkneys, and I had to get the ferry for a twenty-three day stay in the Shetlands. I had to pinch myself sometimes. I was being paid to go to these beautiful places. In the Shetlands, we built dry stone walls on Noss, did footpath work on Unst, fencing and gardening on the mainland, archaeological digging on St Ninian's Isle and various other things.

On Noss, we had some volunteers who had brought musical instruments. There were musical evenings sitting around bonfires on the beach watching the porpoises and seals jumping up out of the sea as if they too were dancing to our music.

I learnt to reverse my horsebox trailer onto all the RO/RO ferries which I thought meant roll on/roll off but really meant reverse on/roll off. I got very adept at driving the Land Rover and trailer around.

On Unst, I had one of the most unforgettably beautiful moments of my life. We were doing some footpath maintenance work on Hermaness Nature Reserve. From there it was possible to see Muckle Flugga and Out Stack – the tiny island which is the most northerly point in the UK. There were panoramic views, and the bright light and the wind gave the sea an ever-changing pattern. On either side of the footpath, there were many burrows in the coarse grass, where puffins lived.

After eating my sandwiches, I stretched out in the sun to take a rest. I had just begun to doze off when I became aware of something beside me. A moment later something on my chest. Two triangles of bright orange. A puffin's feet.

I blinked. The bird stared back with inquisitive eyes,

*Eeh Eeh. Arh.*

Midway between a cows moo and nasal groan. It was a greeting.

"Hello," I replied

*Arh. Eeh. Arh-arh.*

"Is there something you want?"

*Eeeeh.* The sound was emphatic.

"Am I on your burrow? Is that it? Just let me move,"

I shifted to one side. The puffin jumped off and went into the burrow. A moment later it popped back out.

*Eeh. Arh.*

"Not at all. My pleasure."

The bird disappeared into its home. I stayed a few minutes longer, held by the sense of being at one with the island.

It was one of the best moments of my life.

After the last Shetland task it was back to Lerwick for a few days, then a ferry for Aberdeen. I thought, at last, a proper big ferry, the St Magnus, that I can drive straight into. It was just my luck to find that the bow doors were broken and I had to turn the Land Rover and trailer around in about a seventeen point turn, watched by all the laughing lorry drivers, and reverse what felt like miles onto the ship. I became very good at reversing trailers under pressure.

The ferry crossing was very rough, but I had no problems as I just sat in the restaurant and ate lots of proper food, roast chicken and chips, three times I think, mainly as a change to all the tinned stuff I had been eating for two months. I then had another week's holiday but chose to stay in Doune where I had a good rest.

Then it was off once more, first a return to Fairy Glen on the Black Isle for more footpath work. It was very tiring. At the end of this Fairy Glen task, after I had dropped the volunteers off in Inverness, I returned to the accommodation at Rosemarkie. I decided to have a nap for a couple of hours and then go round the local for some beer. I lay down at 6 pm and woke up at 9.30 and thought 'good timing.' I got dressed to go for a pint, but when I went outside, I found it was daylight. It was 9.30 in the morning; I had slept for fifteen and a half hours.

I then made my way over to Skye for a ten-day project camping at Loch Eynort, dry stone walling, and to finish with there were two weeks tree planting on the Isle of Rhum. Six months of absolutely fantastic experiences.

Not one case of depression, I was far too busy for that. Apart from a few parties hardly any beer either. No bad dreams either; at last, I thought I was free of my past.

CHAPTER THIRTEEN

# The importance of a hairy chin

## Sacked again

I returned to the Lakes, unemployed again. I found myself in a situation that I had never been in before. When I tried to sign on for unemployment benefit, I couldn't do so because I couldn't give them an address. At the same time, I couldn't get anywhere to live because I had no money and needed to sign on.

I took the first job I could find, on a building site in the Langdales. The job description asked for a dry stone waller and dumper driver, but when I started I found there was only a couple of metres walling, and I spent the rest of the time trundling around on a 4-tonne dumper. It was a boring job on a badly managed site. But at least it meant I got paid and found somewhere to live, a winter let cottage in Torver, next door to a pub.

I had a few arguments with the building site boss. I managed eight weeks before getting the sack. On my final day, I was using my dumper to fill up a big hole with quarry stone next to the entrance to the site. The delivery wagons were bringing it in, twenty tonnes at a time, entering at the bottom of the hill; driving half a mile up through the site to the top, unloading and then going back for more. Then the digger loaded me up, and I trundled back to the bottom of the site to fill in the hole.

Just after I had dumped a load, a quarry wagon came in. I stopped it and asked the driver if he could drop his load straight into the hole. He was about to do this, when the boss came running down shouting him to stop, and unload in the usual place. I pointed out it made no sense for him to drop twenty tonne at the top of the hill, just for me to bring it back in five loads. His exact words to me were, "Get back on your fucking dumper, and do what I told you; you are not paid to think, you are paid to obey me. Get on your fucking dumper and don't get off until home time."

I took him at his word, and at one point during the afternoon, he walked past me as I was sat on my dumper, smoking a fag, parked in the middle of the road.

"What the fuck are you doing?" he asked.

I said, "I've run out of diesel."

"How come you've done that, it's part of your job to keep it topped up?"

"Well, you told me not to get off the dumper until home time, so how was I supposed to fill up?"

Sacked.

### Self employed at last

I visited the BTCV office on my way home from the building site, wondering what to do next and as I was drinking a cuppa with Charlotte, in walked the National Park Estates Manager. He had heard what I was saying about being jobless and offered me a job as an estate worker. Here was another case of me being in the right place at the right time. It was only for three months; I had to be self-employed for the post, so my work search solved itself. Working with the more experienced estate staff was another good learning experience for me. I worked most of the time with Dave, a bit of a perfectionist. When the three-month contract finished, I carried on working with Dave finding mostly dry stone walling work in the Windermere area for the rest of the year.

At the end of the winter-let season I left the cottage in Torver, moving to live in an old church in Staveley near Windermere. The owners wanted to rent it out to a local worker and were delighted to help out a dry stone waller. In between paid jobs, I kept up my voluntary work with the Conservation Volunteers leading a total of six one-week long working holidays over the year, mainly dry stone walling. I also led some weekend dry stone walling training courses.

In October I had another of those chance meetings which kept me moving on and up in my good life. I attended a chainsaw course over three weekends in Fife in Scotland. I renewed my acquaintance of the folk at the Scottish Conservationists office in Doune. While I was there someone asked me if I was interested in doing some dry stone walling work for the Highland Regional Council the following year. I went to look at the job in December, all the way up to Kinlochhourn, a remote spot on the coast, fifty miles north-west of Fort William. The job entailed rebuilding the sea wall which held up the footpath that ran along the lochside to Barrisdale. I put in a price for the job which was accepted straight away. I don't think there was anyone else daft enough to want to do the job.

1990 began with another unique experience; dry stone walling at Kinlochhourn. My little Ford Escort was not going to be any good for this job so I acquired a cheap old short wheelbase Land Rover for £300 and a trailer. We stayed with Donald, the Deer Stalker at Kinlochhourn. I had three other workers with me, Peter and Paul from the Lakes and a Scottish lad, Dougie, who I'd got to know at Doune.

I told them that I would pay for all the accommodation costs, transport and everything, including £1000 each if we finished the job in four weeks. If it lasted any longer, extra costs would be borne by themselves. The weather was foul at times, but we battled through it all.

We worked our way along the coast, setting off and returning in the dark each day until we got to a one hundred metres long section completely covered in seaweed. We got to work shifting the stuff; it took us all day to clear the footpath. When we returned the next day, the tide had risen so far up that the seaweed was back, one look at it and we all groaned. I said, "Bollocks to this for a game of soldiers", and led the team back to the Land Rover, and drove them all the way to Fort William for a day on the beer. A good session was had by all, made all the more exciting by the fact that, as it had rained all day, the single track road from Invergarry back to Kinlochhourn was flooded in many places. I could only tell where the road edge was by the snow poles. Every time I drove out of the deep water we had to open the doors to let the water out. It was a struggle to keep my foot on the accelerator due to my knees shaking in fear of driving off the road into a loch. A fun, exciting day.

Working in the depths of winter was probably not the best time to work there, but we managed to complete the whole project, over 150 metres of walling and umpteen culvert repairs in the four weeks we were there.

Then it was back to the Lakes once more working with Dave. I traded in my Escort van for a long wheel-based Camper Landrover, complete with a gas cooker, cupboards, sink and a bed. I now had somewhere to live as I made my way around. In April and May, I spent seven weeks back in Scotland working for SCP as a walling instructor on a project to build the entrance walls at the Agricultural Market in

Perth. I kept driving up and down from Scotland to Lakes and during one visit to see Charlotte, she told me about a Project Officers job BTCV were starting up in Carlisle, and she said I should apply for it. I was not sure about it, but I filled in an application form anyway.

Then I stayed up in Scotland picking up work around Glen Lyon, before returning to Kinlochhourn in July to do another three weeks work on more of the sea walls. On this second project, joining me this time were Potter, an ex-miner who lived there and two mates, Chris and John. While we were there, Charlotte came visiting along with John's girlfriend Debbie, from the Ullswater project.

Charlotte told me I had got an interview for the Carlisle job. I couldn't decide if the job was for me. I was enjoying myself being a free agent, though I must admit that it was enjoyable being surrounded by people for most of the time when doing conservation work. Unlike railway gangs, gangs of volunteers generally talked about more interesting subjects than sex. Charlotte and Debbie decided they should tidy me up for the interview by shaving off my beard. It took a whole bottle of whisky to convince me.

I had grown a beard when I was twenty odd, mostly because I couldn't be bothered shaving every day and had never thought of shaving it off. I thought I looked terrible without it, especially the way my white chin contrasted with the other more weather-beaten parts of my face. The girls said I looked twenty years younger and was a new man. They were lying to me though because secretly they too agreed I looked like a chinless plonker.

Without being able to hide behind my beard, during the interview for the BTCV job on 10th August I was far too tense, stressing myself out and I failed to impress. Oh well, I thought, not sure that I wanted it anyway as I didn't want to live in Carlisle.

While I was back in the Lakes I lead another working holiday, dry stone walling up Tongue Ghyll above Grasmere, then I went camping and walking in the Duddon for a few days rest before returning to Scotland to finish a job near Loch Tay. The Scottish midges were hell. I had been straining at my chin for my beard to re-grow as fast as possible to reduce the area of attack from the wee beasties. The next walling job I had in Scotland wasn't until October, so I yo-yo-ed back to the Lakes again to lead another two working holiday weeks working with the far more mild-mannered English midges for a change. I didn't get paid for any of these working holidays, but it did provide me with free food and accommodation.

**Another pay cut**

While I was back in the Lakes, the South Cumbria BTCV Project Officer gave in his notice. This time I readily filled in an application form, thinking that if I got the job, I'd be working in my favourite part of the Lakes. So, on the Friday of the second working holiday, I had another interview for a BTCV job.

The man leading the panel remarked that I seemed entirely different from our last meeting. The truth was that I felt far more relaxed behind my beard again. I knew I wanted the post and convinced them that I was the man for the job. Charlotte was delighted as were all the volunteers on the project and there was much celebrating that Friday night. I started the job on 8th October 1990. My Project Officer's pay of just over £8,000 per year was down on the average £12,000 I made being self-employed. I carried on my business as a dry stone waller throughout my BTCV years to augment my income.

The job was all I wanted it to be, lots of practical work, finding new projects, costing them out, finding and recruiting volunteers, both local and from afar. My assistants were mainly students young and old, some local. These voluntary field officers (VFOs) worked alongside me to get all the work done. Because I hated office work, I could always delegate the paperwork to them. I used to be a little shy in talking to clients when I was a VFO myself, but not now. I knew my stuff. I was in my element, and from the previous years of work, I knew I was able to carry out any form of practical conservation work and also that I could pass on my skills to other people.

Thus I worked through the 90's, year to year, nothing much changed. I did not have sex with anyone nor did I want it. I loved to be in the company of people nowadays and didn't avoid it, but only on my terms. I often left parties and went home, not saying anything to anyone because I didn't want anyone to challenge me. Despite not having any significant depressions, I hated myself internally, and could not work out why so many people kept telling me I was a nice bloke. I wished I could see it myself, but I just couldn't. I just needed to keep my hands busy, and I would be okay.

## CHAPTER FOURTEEN

# *"there is something wrong with me"*

### Home at last

In June 1993, I bought a terraced house in Ulverston. When I counted up the number of times I'd moved over the seven years since leaving Bradford, it came to twelve, so it was appropriate that my house number was thirteen. It is a small two-up-two-down terraced house. I specifically bought it because there isn't a view unless I stand on my tiptoes on my bedroom window ledge where I can just about see The Hoad, a little hill on the outskirts of Ulverston. I once stayed for a year in a rented cottage with lovely views of the mountains. The trouble was, I spent all my time looking and not visiting, taking them for granted. With no view of the hills, I had to get out of the house to see them; once out I am half way to setting foot on them.

I loved my little house and only invited people in occasionally. I would often turn people away when I wasn't in the mood for visitors. I'd tell them I had to go to a meeting or something, or I'd talk to them out in the street. Or just not answer the door. My house didn't just have a front door, but also an invisible stonewall. When, or if, I opened it, you would only get in if you were trusted enough to know how to pass through the wall.

My volunteers and I used to meet up regularly in town for beer, and on my way home I would often berate myself for being responsible for Stephen's death, and wishing I had the courage to kill myself. My memory of his passing was often in my mind, but most of the time I could handle it. Sometimes I couldn't. If one of my bad days coincided with a drinking session, I'd break down crying in front of people and try to explain why I was so miserable. I don't think anyone took me seriously as I always managed to put everything back under wraps as soon as I sobered up. If I was in control, I was all right.

When I was on my own, I could be my whole self. With other people, I had to be just Jerry. I needed to have some close friends I could trust so I could relax in their company. Many of my closest friends came from this decade of my life. I think it must have been hard work especially with my erratic memory, and occasional grumpiness.

I was very utilitarian in the way I decorated my house. I couldn't see the use of lampshades. What was the point of giving light to a room then shading half of it out again? The paint I used reflected my feelings. The entrance room I painted green, with a concrete floor usually filled with tools, materials, stuff in half way transit to the rubbish dump.

In my bedroom, I left the original wallpaper on the walls. It had little bunches of balloons all over it. When one of my friends, Kath, first saw it she said it looked like sperm. The balloons are still there today and will remain till I die. My living room is painted peachy pink and white, my spare room yellow. I have tiled, slate and concrete floors downstairs, and self (i.e. badly) fitted carpets upstairs. It is my house, my muck, my dust. I am happy with it, and above all, that is what counts.

My parents only ever visited my house once; as soon as he got in, my dad started criticised my decorating, so they were driven out, neither of them to set foot in my house ever again.

During the years after I moved out of my parents' house, I occasionally popped back to Keighley to stay with them. Sometimes we met up in the Lakes when they brought their caravan up. I sent my mum a letter in 1986, telling her once and for all that I was gay, and to please accept it. I told her that I didn't need either of them in my life; unless they agreed to stop using the phrase 'God's good' at the end of every single conversation I had with them, I wouldn't speak to them again.

I hated them saying it; reminding me of my past and it angered me. I pleaded with my parents to stop doing it, but they never did. Finally, I told them both one day that I hated their religion and their God, and if they said 'GG' to me again, I would tell them to fuck off. Then they started saying, "I know you are going to swear at me for saying this but, God's good." "Fuck. . . Off." It was almost as if they had been programmed to keep saying it.

Whenever my mum rang my office, if a female volunteer answered the phone, later my mum would ring me at home to say to me, "She sounds like a lovely girl, you have got some nice girls working with you." She never called me when a man answered the phone. I know they didn't like me as myself so I mostly kept out of the way, and only visited Keighley to see Stuart for drinking sessions and to stock up on the curry spices I couldn't buy in the Lakes.

My practical work went on merrily but slowly, as these things tend to do, the paperwork required to carry out the job increased every year. Most of the time I could off-load this onto my helpers, but not all. When I started the job, I was working outside four or five days a week, but this was gradually whittled down to less than two. I had to spend more time in the office sitting at a table where my concentration started to drift. I'd flashback to my maths exam, the aversion therapy and I got more and more depressed.

I was expected to remember more stuff, and I knew I was hopeless at learning through academic means. Doing practical work was automatic. I knew what I was doing and why, but the admin was completely lost on me. Then the computer arrived, supposedly to make things easier but as with most new things, no one thought it right to give me any tuition. I tried to avoid having one, but eventually, they foisted one on me. I got to hating that computer. It produced far more paperwork than ever before. The worst thing was, rather than people ringing me up to discuss things, I got emails. It was almost as if what head office wanted in my post was not a brilliant practical worker who could do a bit of admin, but an admin officer who would kowtow to all these other admin types who ran the Trust.

One of my duties as Project Officer was to make enough money for the people in head office to be paid lots of money to drive around the country looking pretty. If we had got rid of the lot of them and been minimalist in our overheads, we wouldn't have had to charge so much for our work.

As I felt myself slowly getting more depressed, another of those confusing memories popped into my head. I remembered getting out of a car at the mental hospital carrying my school bag. I do not know why, because I never got a lift to the hospital. I always did the fifteen-minute walk. I never took my schoolbag with me.

I went to see my GP and told her I was depressed and asked her to look through my medical records to see if there was anything about the AT. She found a letter from the mental hospital referring me for AT from June 1972. She then put me down to see the mental health people.

I attended an appointment with a psychiatrist on the 16th November 1998, for a mental health assessment. The following is an excerpt from the letter sent to my GP:

> *'Indeed his experiences have been unfortunate and tragic. The aversion therapy has been traumatic in itself, and as you rightly mention, Jeremy never had a chance to grieve over the death of his boyfriend. He became quite tearful when he said: "there is something wrong with me," in what appeared to be a core negative belief about himself which is a result of the aversion therapy. I recommend therapy for Post-Traumatic Stress Disorder and unresolved grief. I have put him on the waiting list with high priority.'*

I was such a high priority that I had to wait until 22nd September 1999 before my therapy began. This wasn't like in the seventies when it only took two weeks from seeing my GP to the first electric shock. I did not get to read this letter until 2011.

During the time I was having therapy, I continued at work. I was deeply indebted to my co-workers who kept the office going while my mind was elsewhere. Vickie, Lou, Cath, Glen, Shaun and Andrew, all deserve medals as big as dustbin lids. I must have been hell to work with, on edge all the time.

Having to think about the past brought back more memories. I had a lot of blank spots in my memory banks regarding the AT. I remembered the electric shocks and the showing of pictures, but there were still odd memories which didn't make sense. Arriving at the mental hospital by car already confused me, and I got the feeling that I woke up in a bed in the mental hospital.

My brother Neil, rang me up one day when I was feeling especially down, but I couldn't talk to him. I told him I was depressed. A few hours later he turned up at my door wanting to know why I was depressed. I told him all about being gay, the AT, and Stephen. He didn't know anything about any of it. He wanted to know if our parents knew, and I said I hadn't told them about the AT or Stephen, but they knew I was gay but they wouldn't accept my sexuality.

He stated that they must have known about the AT, and wanted to drive down immediately to sort them out. We visited our parents the following weekend. Neil asked them if they knew anything about the AT. They denied all knowledge of it and said if they had known they would have stopped it. When I told them that the priests at school had told me not to tell them about it, they just agreed that should not have happened. My dad said, "It is too late to do anything about it now." Maybe I should have told them years ago, but at least they knew now. I hoped that they would do me a favour and stop insisting that their God was good for me.

In early 2000 I began to feel that I couldn't keep going to therapy and continue doing my job. I took four weeks off on sick leave and went dry stone walling up the Duddon. The worksite was high up Long House Gill by the Walna Scar track below Dow Crag. I was working on my own, doing what I was good at with absolutely no paperwork. Though it was February, the weather was kind to me. I thoroughly enjoyed myself; I was in my kind of heaven.

On my return to work, I asked my line manager, Charlotte, if I could have unpaid leave for six months to try and get my head sorted out. Initially, BTCV refused but later changed their mind. However, after just one week off, I gave my one month's notice and left BTCV. Ten years previously

I thought I had got the perfect job for my life. But my past had caught up with me once more; I found myself running away again. But at least this time I was returning to my beloved dry stone walling work.

Throughout my years with BTCV, I had kept myself registered as self-employed with the Tax Office. I augmented my income by about £2000 a year doing dry stone walling jobs around the South Lakes. I also got all my certification to become an Agricultural Training Board Trainer. This allowed me to get paid a day-rate for training courses in outdoor conservation skills; dry stone walling, fencing, hedgelaying and footpath work.

I had a good reputation as a dry stone waller so I was quite successful in finding enough work. Some of the BTCV volunteers that I had taught to wall went self-employed. Now they returned the favour by passing some work my way.

CHAPTER FIFTEEN

# The itch

My therapy continued weekly until 9th August 2000. I had forty-one one-hour sessions spending an awful lot of the time in having grief counselling for the loss of Stephen.

At the end of the therapy, I felt that all of my issues had been addressed. I talked extensively about my childhood; my parents and events surrounding Stephen's death. They convinced me that I was not to blame for his death. It was just an accident. I had to keep telling myself this though, I was still not sure whether I believed it. My fear was that to get out of my depression, I had to lose Stephen, to forget him and move on. This conflicted with my need to keep him in my mind. I feared being left with nobody if I let Stephen go for a new relationship and it did not succeed. I was determined to find a way to keep my love for him. I re-focused my thoughts of Stephen to just the happy ones.

The psychologists didn't go deeply into the effects that the aversion therapy may have had on me. No-one seemed willing to discuss anything about it. They unanimously agreed that it was traumatic, but it was mostly left alone. I must admit the most traumatic event of my life was watching Stephen die and I think they just concentrated on that.

Around the time the therapy was finishing, I developed an itch in my right forearm. A very irritating itch. Ordinary everyday irritations were annoying but responded to the odd scratch and maybe a bit of antiseptic. This itch was different. It was a persistent pain which went right along the outside of my right arm, between my wrist and my elbow. After withstanding it for a few weeks, I went to visit my GP. She couldn't find anything wrong with my arm. She thought it might be an allergy, so I did lots of tests, but the itch just continued. I tried all sorts of dermatitis creams, all to no avail. Sometimes I had to scrape the creams off as they made the pain worse.

The itch got so bad that I couldn't sleep. I found it difficult to concentrate. I scratched at my arm endlessly, to the point of using wire washups which stripped the skin off my arm, but nothing worked. I tried to keep my left hand firmly in my pocket, but I just could not stop the temptation to scratch. Scabs often covered my arm as my fingernails ripped into my skin. I took to wearing tubular bandages so I could continue to scratch my arm without causing blood to flow. In desperation, my GP put me on a repeat prescription of antihistamines which if nothing else at least helped me sleep.

In the end, I just learnt to accept it and add it to the other aches that all too often caused me pain. I had unexplained strange pains in my right shoulder and neck, which felt tight or strained, but here again despite x-rays and examinations there didn't seem to be anything wrong with my shoulder.

I noticed there were times when these pains went away; I could live my life without them. These were when I was working hard; walling, working out in the hills and fields; when I was driving, out rock climbing, or walking. When I was doing these things, I felt in control of my life. I felt strangely complete and at peace.

But back at home watching telly, reading, washing up, mundane tasks or in the pub, the arm itch would come back with a vengeance. People probably thought I had fleas.

Work was going well. Memorable work sites included walls on the top of Ingleborough and high up above Seathwaite Tarn in the Duddon Valley. The Duddon was always my favourite valley and I was lucky that I found so much work there. When I am dead and gone I will have left my mark all over the Lake District, but mostly in the Duddon.

My old V reg series three Landrover had been struggling for a while, especially with the amount of off-road driving I was doing up and down the Walna Scar track. I started contemplating buying a new one when in February 2001 the Foot and Mouth epidemic struck. I went from having a full order book to having no work in a matter of days. Farmers didn't want people going from farm to farm working. There was a lot of talk about all the poor tourist places losing out, but no-one seemed to think about the people who worked the land who were not farmers.

Charlotte's husband, Tim, suggested that I put an advert in the Westmorland Gazette. The ad had the headline 'Dry stone waller out of work due to Foot and Mouth requires garden walling work.' This advert cost me £150 and brought in about £35,000's worth of work which kept me, and a few mates, who were also affected by the F&M, going for the whole period of the outbreak. One of the jobs was in Garsdale, forty odd miles away in the Yorkshire Dales, which quickly took a toll on the old Landy.

In April I bought a two-year-old LWB Defender for £11,222 for which I took out a loan. So from a position of wondering what I was going to do about work and worrying about my finances, I was okay again. When the F&M died down, I went back to my farm and hillside walling work.

One of the people who came to work with me was Ness, who in 1991 was among my earliest VFO's. I had taught her how to dry stone wall; she was so good at it that she went self-employed for a while before moving away. Now she had moved back to Barrow, and we started working together.

Now the psychotherapy was over I decided to see if I could do something about trying to find any information about the Aversion Therapy. Mostly my thoughts about the AT had taken a back seat due to the trauma of Stephen's death. I couldn't remember anything about most of it. But I had strangely disconnected memories about it. One was arriving by car with my school bag when I can only ever remember walking there without my bag. Another was of me waking up in the hospital as I only remember day-visits. I wanted to meet other people who went through my experience and to see if I could fill in any of the blanks in my memory.

I saw an article in the Gay Times asking for anyone who had had AT to get in touch with the Wellcome Trust as they were doing research on it. I rang them and a doctor, G, arranged to visit me at home to take an 'oral history' about my experiences. He said they were going to produce a book about AT, about both the health professionals and the patients they treated.

Later on, G rang me up again and asked if I wanted to do a BBC Radio 4 programme called 'All in the Mind' with Raj Persaud about AT. I jumped at the chance because again I thought I would find details about the treatment that other people received. I went down to London in July, 2001, to do the programme. Though the whole experience was okay, I was very nervous, the itch didn't help either, but everyone involved helped me along. The programme went out, and I hoped something good for me would happen, but I am afraid nothing came of it. The Wellcome Trust never produced a book, there is a website about it, but I was disappointed. At no time did I ever get to meet anyone who had had AT. After this, drawing on the results of my earlier therapy, I just let it all go, it was all in the past now, and I decided to move on. My depressions were over.

In my desire to move on, I started doing Spanish lessons. An idea I had was to go abroad. I quite liked the idea of going to South America, where Spanish is spoken in most countries. The Spanish language courses went well. So well in fact that I booked a trip to Costa Rica for six weeks to do a language course in the capital, San Jose. But then something happened just before I went to Costa Rica that didn't stop me going but would put me off going abroad again for a very long time.

CHAPTER SIXTEEN

# Love's a bitch

In August 2001, I was working on a farm in the Duddon valley where the resident sheepdog had had some puppies. They were a gorgeous cross between a brown labrador dog and a collie bitch. There were seven when I started work, and these were slowly whittled down to two as they were sold off. These two used to follow me about, and I decided to buy one. As they were both lovely, I decided that the one that stays with me longest has chosen me, so that is the one I will have.

I picked her up on 8th September as a 48th birthday present to myself. I called her Boady, as the farm was called Boadhole. Not a good name in some respects as I was forever being asked if she was named after Bodie from a TV programme, The Professionals. So now I have a dog. She was completely unplanned. When I went to Costa Rica for my holiday, Boady had to live with a friend for a while.

My holiday in Costa Rica was fantastic. I stayed at the home of a Costa Rican family. They were not allowed to talk to me in English and this they did so well that it wasn't until my last but one day that they spoke to me in English, which was far better than my Spanish. They must have spent every day trying not to laugh at my silly dependence on a Spanish dictionary. On arrival at the airport in San Jose, I got a taxi into the city. I struggled to talk to the driver in my new language. As luck would have it, six weeks later I got the same driver back to the airport when I left. He congratulated me as we talked in Spanish.

I thought it was marvellous at the school that a group of entirely different language speakers could converse with each other in one common language. I went to a restaurant with a Japanese lad, a Swiss woman and a French couple and we were able to speak to each other albeit hesitantly, in our new language.

On each weekend, I set out to visit different parts of Costa Rica. On the second weekend I drank beer, sitting at a beach bar and swam in the Caribbean; on the third, I drank beer at a beach bar and swam in the Pacific. Then on the fourth, I stayed at a hotel in the centre of the country next to an erupting volcano, Mount Arenal. Here I found the luxury of sitting in the warm sunshine, cooling myself in a swimming pool with a circular bar in the middle of it. Mount Arenal was covered in cloud when I got to the hotel and I was wondering what all the fuss was about. Later that day the weather cleared so I spent much of the evening drinking beer watching the lava coming down the mountain.

I did spend some time enjoying the countryside without the beer. I experienced enough fear during a Canopy Zip Wire tour that kept me going for years. The tour involved eleven zips, over about three kilometres. They started at the top of a mountain and the cables got longer each time. Zipping through the forest from platform to platform was exhilarating. Then one wire led me out of the trees across an open ravine and a waterfall. My knees were knocking as I arrived at the next platform. The safety guides kept joking about the last and longest zip, all eight hundred metres of it. I thought they were just ribbing me, telling me that I had to complete the last zip otherwise I would have to walk back up the mountain to the starting point.

The last zip was probably more frightening than anything I have ever done. The first fifty metres through the canopy were okay, but then you fly out into the open, hundreds of metres above the ground. Coming towards me rapidly was a cliff that I thought I was going to hit and as I started screaming at the top of my voice, the cable went safely past it, down and down to the finish. After I was untied from the cable, much to the amusement of everyone there, I collapsed on my knees and kissed the ground.

When I got back and went to pick up Boady, she bounced all around me, and from then on I would never be alone again. When people asked me if I was lonely living on my own, I could say, "No, there is always some Boady with me." I fell in love with her, and she fell in love with the food I gave her. Since I did not want to leave her, I lost my interest in going abroad, by plane without her again.

Throughout my life, I had various accidents and illnesses, but as I got older, I started to accumulate longer term body problems. Throughout this period I had the evilly painful arm itch, but to add to it in October 2002, I received cortisone injections in both elbows to help me with my Tennis elbow, a result of too much chainsawing, stone lifting, and probably excessive pint lifting too.

In March 2003, I managed to get cancer of the tongue. I will always know in future if I have anything awful wrong with me, by the way hospital staff treated me with regards to my cancer. It started as a little ulcer in my mouth that wouldn't go away, so I went to my GP looking for antibiotics. After one look she referred me straight to the hospital for a biopsy. When I attended my appointment, I just joined the queue like everyone else, patiently waiting my turn. After they had chopped a few bits out of my mouth, they asked me to come back the following week. On my return as soon as I had registered, a nurse came to take me straight in, bypassing the waiting room, to see the doctor who told me about my cancer. It did make me fearful, all the horrible stories you hear about cancer, but I needn't have worried. The NHS came to my rescue.

In April I had an operation in Preston to chop a lump off my tongue. Waking up in the hospital after the operation, I was very agitated and was again told by the nurses it was just the anaesthesia wearing off. I thought about telling doctors about me being allergic to anaesthetic as it was always being blamed for my agitation when waking up. I also thought I was in a room by myself, but when talking about my hospital stay with some friends who visited me, they told me that I was in the ward with other patients, so I don't know where that thought came from. Just another strange enigma to add to all the rest. It took just five weeks from visiting my GP, discovering the cancer and having the operation.

I decided that Boady must visit the tops of all my beloved Lakeland fells. Over the years I had already done all the 214 fells listed in Wainwright's books. I started visiting them all again but now accompanied by Boady. She was a Stephen-send to me, a black haired beauty who followed, or ran barking madly around me across the tops in rain, snow and sunshine. She started with Green Crag on the 25th of May 2003 and finished with Castle Crag on the 5th of September 2010.

I celebrated my 50th birthday in September 2003 with a mega-party. I booked a pub in Broughton, hired a band, and invited everyone (that I liked and could find) from my past. It was a great success and much (for me far too much) alcohol was drunk. It was great to see all my old rock climbing mates, BTCV friends, Keighley and college friends.

Work was going very well, working now full time with Ness. My life had settled down once more to a good time with me fully involved in walking the fells with my pooch, working hard, and generally, I think, the therapy had helped me get on with life.

In late 2004, I was contacted again by Dr G from the Wellcome Trust, who asked me if I was willing to do a TV programme about AT. After a lot of thought I said yes and on 7th January 2005, I went down to London to do the programme. We did the filming at a pub in Belgravia. After the filming Andrew, one of my old BTCV mates, took me out for a night on the town. I kept in touch with the BBC, and finally, the programme was aired on BBC2 on 9th August 2005. Called 'Sad to be Gay' it told the story of one gay man's search to try and 'cure' himself of his homosexuality. My bit was just a two-minute interview (which took two hours and five pints to film) about my experiences during the AT. As with my reasoning for doing the Radio 4 interview in 2001, I agreed to the programme in the hope of finding someone who had had the aversion therapy but again nothing came of it. On the day before the programme went out, I was rung up by a journalist from the Times who asked me if I would do an interview for them to publish in their paper. I agreed with the understanding that I would be kept anonymous.

The next day the article was published with my full name included. I was very upset by this because while I knew I had been on telly, not many of our work clients would be likely to see it. This was a different matter when it came to the newspaper article. We got all our walling work from my name, (and Ness's brilliance) so if anyone wanted to find me, they could use a search engine to find me. Now, when my name was searched for, there were two entries using my full name, one as a dry stone walling contractor in Cumbria; the other the Times article about a gay man who did countryside work in Cumbria. People may think that I was over-reacting to the importance of this but up here in Cumbria live some of the most homophobic people you could wish never to meet. This was not the big city where gay people were more accepted, this was a rural area where I was definitely not 'out', and I wanted to keep it that way.

This incident stressed me out again, and I slipped back into depression. This time I didn't want to wait another twelve months for an NHS appointment, so I popped into my local Mind office where I met a counsellor called Shirley. So started another course of psychotherapy which lasted until the end of the year. This time it wasn't as bad as in the past; Shirley proved to be brilliant. I saw her weekly until late December, and at the end, I wrote in my diary "Shirley has done a lot for me to lift me up from hopefully my last depression." In one case in particular, she made me think entirely differently about my experiences.

CHAPTER SEVENTTEN

# Stephen's pentagram

One thing I have not mentioned in my story so far, is the pentagram that Stephen gave me. It is an open pentagram with no circle around it. It weighs fifty grams and measures three inches between the points. Stephen made the star for me, and I just accepted it as a gift from my friend. I have kept it close to me all my life. It hangs next to my fireplace where I see it every day; I often wear it when I am meditating.

At some point during a long therapy session with Shirley, I mentioned the pentagram. She was immediately interested, and told me that I ought to go online to see what it means if someone gives you a gift of a pentagram. Shirley had done some studying into Wiccan ideas and recognised the meaning of the pentagram.

That evening I searched for information online. The answers I got changed my whole outlook on life. I'd never fully understood the significance of Stephen's present. I now found that Stephen may have given it to me to protect me from evil. Has it worked? I feel that it has, maybe it was responsible for me being in the right place at the right time so often as I have changed directions in life. Maybe it provided me with the strength to keep going when I was on the verge of suicide

As I looked into the meaning of the pentagram, I discovered Paganism. Maybe this was the idea, that I had to wait until now to find its meaning. Now I could use it to help me going forward. Without the pentagram, I would not have discovered Wicca and hence moved towards the Tarot and paganism. I am not sure I was searching for an alternative religion to follow, but paganism seemed to suit my thoughts. I continued seeing Shirley for a while with weekly meetings, and I fought my way out of my depression yet again.

I found a statement about Fate. Fate is not about how I am going to die, not a fatality. Fate is a force inherently existing within me, driving me to act in a certain way, to feel attracted to certain things rather than others. It was my fate to become a dry stone waller. Understanding the pentagram could give me the means to find myself so that I could make myself the master of my life rather than the victim of it.

There have often been times when I've felt some form of spiritual experience walking in the countryside. I just ignored these events as being silly. One day on Widdop, in the South Pennines, I got a weird feeling that I was surrounded by spirits. It was one of those days where the sun shone through the clouds; I was surrounded by strange lights and shades, a good feeling.

Another thought I had was that Stephen made the star for Jeremy, not Jerry. So if I were to follow what I perceived were the intentions of Stephen giving me the gift, I should be in the mind of Jeremy.

Using the power of the pentagram, I started to try and pick up on these feelings and see what they could mean for me. Looking back I felt this has happened many times in the Lakes, always on my own though; up a valley between Gray Crag and Hartsop Dodd I felt the pull of the rock face; finding a hidden footpath on the way up Scafell Pike; in the Beacon fells above Coniston Lake; standing in a waterfall below the Crinkle Crags.

One day, as I was making my way through some very thick tangled bracken struggling to find a way out, I saw a little bird swooping just off to my left side, almost saying, "this way Jeremy," and in another few strides in its direction, I was out in the open. I didn't know until later that little birds tend to fly around in openings, I just knew freedom would come if I went towards the bird.

Walking through the woods; smelling the flowers of the larch trees, my senses seem to be far more alive than I ever thought them capable. I tried to relate the five elements that are associated with the five points of the pentagram: Air, Earth, Fire, Water and Spirit with my experiences. A windy, wet walk related to an air/water walk, a sunny day walking barefoot in the hills was sensed as a fire/earth walk. I found that when I tried to experience the countryside as much as I could all my negative thoughts about my past receded.

There then followed probably some of my most enjoyable adult years. I read books on witchcraft. I discovered a Wiccan writer called T.Thorn Coyle. She writes beautifully. Taking me away into hidden worlds. I bought a Universal Waite Tarot Deck and the book 'Learning the Tarot' by Joan Bunning. She says one should try to feel what the card means to you first before reading the meanings of the cards.

When I first opened my Tarot pack, I shuffled the cards, saying to myself 'what are the meanings these cards have for me? The card I drew was the Page of Pentacles, which shows a man holding a pentagram in his hands gazing up at it. The man is standing in a field with woods and mountains behind him. He is wearing green and brick red, two of my favourite colours. I thought this is me, holding up Stephen's pentagram trying to figure out what it means. Then I read the description, 'revel in the delights of being alive on the Earth at this time,' 'be practical' and 'work with what you have.'

I reshuffled the cards, and thought to myself, the next card I picked out would represent Stephen in all my future readings. The card I turned up this time really blew me away and proved to me the strength of these cards. I didn't need to read the book to see what the card meant to me. The Eight of Pentacles depicts a young man sitting on a bench making a pentagram. I was now hooked on the meanings of the Tarot and whenever I needed an answer to a question I would ask the Tarot. Over the next few years, it proved indispensable to me.

In the past, I had tried meditation but not got very far with it, but now I tried it again. This time a more Wiccan variety with thoughts based on the pentagram and the Elements. I was open to experiencing whatever I needed to, to stop me falling back into depression. I started to do meditation walks in a local wood, or around my favourite hills, meditating as I walked using my senses to experience emotions. Emotions – energy in motion. I'd sit still in different places and slowly go through the Elements and their associations and tried to experience whatever was going on. I developed these meditations over the years as I learnt more about the Elements.

In one incredible week in May, I spent a holiday in Wales in the company of Vickie, Lou and Cath. These were the Girly Gang, three women who helped me run the BTCV office in the late 1990's. Lots of hugging, yakking with a bunch of beautiful people. Lovely people, lovely time. While on Anglesey I spent some time visiting ancient tombs and stone circles in the search for spiritual experiences. Best memory, Vickie playing her penny whistle as I drove slowly along the back-roads of Anglesey in the sunshine. What an Absolutely Brilliant Fantastic Week's Holiday.

I further cheered myself up by making a will. I stated that I must not be buried in any Catholic way. I wanted to be cremated and my ashes buried with the pentagram. I gave a grid reference of one of my walls in the Duddon valley where I would like my ashes to be placed.

I'd hopefully made sure that Catholics wouldn't have anything to do with my funeral.

2006 found me continuing Boady's Wainrights, achieving 36 of them. On our walk up Carrock Fell, north of Keswick the weather was beautiful; there wasn't a cloud in the sky until a little cloud appeared, so I said "I did not order that" and the little cloud promptly disappeared.

I joined a Wicca group called Shared Earth in Preston. I attended an Incense Making workshop. I had a great time. I started collecting many different types of stone to represent the five elements. I bought a stone topped table on which I made myself a little altar, and accumulated lots of oils, herbs and resins for making my incense. I put together a pentagram incense and oil. I started staying in more, drinking less and sitting in my room burning incense and reading. I joined another Wiccan group based in Lancaster. I got on well with all these pagans, and I found it was more a way of life and living than a formal religion.

I spent much of my spare time studying paganism; going to local groups and gatherings. I can honestly say that I always felt welcomed where ever I went by Wiccan folk. I was also open about my sexuality. In my time I have studied the various religions of the world, and I believe they all say more or less the same regarding the sinfulness of gay people, but personally I only found it was pagans who practiced what they preached, not that they really preached anything anyway.

I continued searching out the stone circles that are scattered around the Lakes, visiting them during my frequent big walks. I felt fantastically happy roaming the fells off the path, occasionally standing naked under waterfalls and shouting out loud my love for Stephen. I thanked him for making me, as I am, a loner yes, but being free to do my thing in my own way.

I finally let all my depressions about Stephen go, and I began to cherish knowing him. I know I am obsessed with him and some may criticise me for not releasing that obsession. Now with the help of Shirley and many good friends I had found a form of relative peace.

CHAPTER EIGHTEEN

# Watching the trees grow

On most worksites Ness and I would work together, but I still preferred working on my own. Ness couldn't work without listening to Radio One and her endlessly beeping mobile phone. How come nowadays people are so addicted to talking to their mates all day? I reckon the amount of work done in a day has fallen dramatically since the invention of the mobile phone. Her statement about my mobile not going off at work was that I was Mister-No-Mates. My own view was that if someone wants to ring me, they can do so on my home phone and leave a message. I hated talking into my mobile for more than a few seconds as it made my arms ache.

Another mismatch between Ness and me was that I always preferred working in remote places and didn't like garden walls. We still did garden walls, as we usually got paid more. I sometimes found it hard to justify charging more for garden walls. If, whenever I build a wall anywhere I always build it to my highest standard, why should I need to charge more in a garden? I'm obviously not a capitalist.

Working on my own, I could watch the wildlife and revel in being where I was. Even with Boady for company I was still mostly on my own as my darling doggy often went off for hours at a time doing her own thing. She always came back at break times though, as she sensed from afar that food might be available.

Often I would meditate, and I treasured the quieter places. I could just sit, relax and watch the trees grow. I get a real feeling of peace if I follow my instincts when I am walling as the stones slot into place perfectly. I like to think I learnt to build walls by absorbing into my body the atoms from the hands of the long forgotten wallers who built these walls originally.

In March 07, I got another call from Dr G from the Wellcome Trust, asking me if I was interested in doing another programme about Aversion Therapy. This would be for Channel 4. This time, after very little thought, I decided against it. I remembered what had happened after the last TV programme and, having dragged myself once more out of my deep depression, I had no urge to return. I had given up on trying to find other people to talk to who had experienced AT. The original Wellcome Trust project had produced no results, and the book they said they were going to produce never appeared. I had found a level of contentment and did not want to risk losing it.

Work was going very well with some good projects all around the Lakes. Our clients were farmers in all the valleys of South Lakes, the National Trust, and the odd private company. During May to October 2007, we carried out a project on the Caw to Haycock ridge, 2100 feet plus above Ennerdale. The remote nature of the site meant we needed to stay on site as the daily commute of over an hour's drive each way, and three hours' walk up and down to the site, just wouldn't have been feasible. The Forestry Commission helicoptered up a portacabin, storage hut, one tonne of bottled water, loads of tools, food and equipment to keep us going for five months. We decided to work a four-day week. As we were staying on site, it meant we'd achieve the same number of hours work in four days as we would normally do in five. I really looked forward to the work as I was fulfilling three of my favourite pastimes in one: walling, walking, and being in the mountains.

We started 15th May and finished 28th September, completing seventy-four days over nineteen weeks. On thirty-one of those days it rained all day, on fifteen days we had sunshine with no clouds, and all the rest it was mostly misty, showery or gloomy and nearly always windy. After a couple of very wet weeks, we got a lovely sunny week. The only trouble was, the hot weather coincided with no wind and the midges made life so bad we prayed for the wind to come back. Then, one stormy night, it was so windy that the metal spikes that were holding the portacabin in place moved about six inches, a frighteningly moving experience.

We only had two of my friends who came to stay the night, both bringing whiskey, which helped pass the time. My brother, Neil, came up to visit us but couldn't find where we were and left a bottle of beer in amongst some rocks on Red Pike (three miles away) which I didn't retrieve until after the project had finished. The project objective was for 450 metres of which we completed 435 which was an average of just under six completed per day. The main reason we got so much done was that on rainy days there was nothing else to do but suffer from cabin fever, which gave us the energy to get outside and chuck rocks about.

There were a few times over the years when we nearly ran out of work and then others when we had a couple of years' work ahead. During the slack times, we just worked slower and made the work last rather than running out completely. Then something else would appear out of the blue, and we would be off working a five day week again.

Things just carried on for the next few years. I had the usual confusions in my head when I got too drunk and felt a bit down, but life was going too well to let anything spoil my happiness. Highlights of 2008 included spending the Grand National weekend in Blackpool visiting Funny Girls and gay pubs. Beautiful work sites included Blea tarn in Langdales, Tarn Hows, Duddon Valley, Hutton Roof and the top of Farleton fell.

I joined a local meditation group, had lots of long walks in the mountains in rain and sun, and in total, I spent 274 days of 2008 either working, walking or both at the same time. Towards the end of the year, we made the first contact with Holker Hall who would provide us with the bulk of our dry stone walling work for the next few years.

## Old Friends

I got back in touch with my friends who were far flung around Britain. I found my old rock climbing pal Eileen lived in the North Lakes, so was not too far away for a visit. Eileen suggested I looked into Shamanism. Shamanism is the most ancient spiritual practice known to humankind dating back at least 40,000 years. Shamanism teaches us that everything that exists is alive and has a spirit. I feel this spirit when I am out walking. A shaman is a man or woman who goes into an altered state of consciousness and travels outside of time into the hidden realms. Residing in these hidden realms, there are compassionate spirits who offer their guidance and also their healing help on behalf of all life on earth.

One of the most common types of spirits are power animals. Travelling into the hidden realms is called journeying. In early 2009, I attended a Shamanic Journeying course where I found my power animal. I was wondering who or what it may be when I heard what sounded like a poorly cow behind me. "Eeeeh Arrgh." and met my puffin friend from Hermaness Nature Reserve in the Shetlands, and I felt I had the perfect power animal. The next day when I journeyed into the upper world, I felt I had a pronounced out of body experience. It was a bit weird as I seemed to be able to journey reasonably easily. I put this down to my meditations and the opening up of my spiritual side.

CHAPTER NINETEEN

# The three plunge routine

On 10th March 2009 I woke up, swung myself out of bed in my usual manner, ending up sitting on the side of my bed facing the wall. Staring at my feet I felt weird, my head still, my eyes moving but not seeing anything. I had a completely blank mind. It was as if some of my senses had stopped working. Looking at my hands, I could see them but I couldn't sense them. My breathing was very shallow. I felt detached as my mind wandered around inside my head. I don't know how long this went on for. It was only when I got anxious and started to shake that I seemed to break the spell. A strange cramping in my stomach. Slowly I worked out where I was, and who I was, and my memories slowly returned.

One of the first thoughts to return was my love for Stephen, aching for him, but in pain at his loss. Why did I always associate love with pain? In a panic, I booked an appointment with my GP, but cancelled it later as I couldn't think how I was going to explain it.

## Getting closer to nature

During my walks around the mountains, I started walking barefoot. This was another way I could experience the sensation of the Element Earth. I felt sensually alive to all my surroundings when out in the fells. Walking up Grey Friar from Seathwaite tarn, in the Duddon Valley, I set off early. The icy ground felt cold beneath my bare feet, but as I climbed the hill, the sun slowly warmed up the earth, and it was a beautiful experience to feel the warmth of the grass beneath my feet. I was able to sense the Elements of both Earth and Fire on my feet. I didn't just walk the grassy fells; I also topped off Crinkle Crags, Scoat Fell and Steeple amongst the forty two fells completed barefoot in 2009.

On one long walk, I reflected that I was a very lucky person. I have been in love most of my life. I was sixteen when I fell in love with Stephen, and now I love my Boady, I love the Lake District hills, I love experiencing nature. I love all those wonderful people I have had the privilege of meeting over the years. When I got home I drew two Tarot cards to describe my feelings for the day, the first was the Lovers, and the other was the Five of Cups, the card of suffering loss, and feeling sorrow. These Tarot cards sometimes cheered me up, and at other times made me feel sad. As I looked further into the meaning of the Five of Cups, it read that one could feel deprived of love and have a longing to be re-united. Oh I wish.

Mid August 2009 brought the first of a few more aches and pains which were to hit my body over the following years. I developed an awful itchy bum infection which meant walking was akin to having a bunch of razor blades up there. I had always suffered from painful cramps in my thighs after hard exercise, be that playing rugby or fellwalking, but these got more extreme, making it difficult to walk the day following an attack. I spent some time visiting doctors and nurses trying to figure out what was wrong. My prostate was all right, cholesterol levels too high, blood pressure all right. The whole thing led me to getting some bum cream, which despite my name for it, worked quite well. A change of diet too, more fruit, veg and granary bread. Problem solved.

Towards the end of the year, the weather just got wetter and wetter until one day in November it rained all day very heavily, resulting in floods all over Cumbria. Roads blocked, bridges washed away, a policeman died, it was a terrible time.

Then in mid-December snow fell very deeply. It lingered long and hard. Typically the snow would be gone in a couple of days, but this lot didn't go until mid-January. What with all the floods and snow, we only managed to get to work for twenty-four days in three months. When we did get back to work in February 2010, we had a lovely month of sunshine completing 120 metres of wall on top of Humphrey Head overlooking Morecambe Bay.

## My house

One disadvantage of living a long time in a small terrace house is that one's next door neighbours keep changing. As my luck would have it, coinciding with me trying to turn my life around, a new set of neighbours threatened to turn my life back into the depths of another depression. They were the noisiest neighbours possible, who besides having very long loud parties every other night, also had a full drum kit in the bedroom next to mine. They played these drums at all sorts of times during the day and night. I was finding it difficult not to be angry at home, and meditation became impossible.

I complained to the council and the police about them but nothing changed. I was in danger of getting very depressed. I had to do something. As I was wondering what to do, even considering moving house, I got a lovely surprise. I got a check for £2,300 for compensation after being mis-sold payment protection insurance for the loan I used to buy my Landrover in 2001.

On entering my house from the street, you came into an open room, which was difficult to keep warm. So, using this compensation money, I had a sound-proofed partition wall put up. This made the room only eight foot by ten foot. I had the floor tiled with slate, and as I had already installed stone shelves and a stone fireplace years ago, I now had a cosy (for me!) room. Well suited to a stoneman. I found a lady online who made woollen rugs to order. I had her make me a five foot square black wool rug, embellished with a large grey pentagram, which I laid on the floor of the stoneroom. This became my magic meditation room. Back in control again, my depression lifted.

In June 2010 my bum pain came back with a vengeance, closely followed by a terrible stomach ache. I got some more cream for my bum, but the pain in my stomach just got worse by the day. So started a long summer of visits to nurses, doctors and hospitals. In July I had to visit Furness General for a gastroscopy where they pushed a camera down my throat to see what was causing my stomach aches and they found I had a Hiatus Hernia and a stomach ulcer. They told me I should avoid bending over and make sure I didn't lift anything too big. Good advice for a dry stone waller! Then in amongst all the blood tests, I got told I have type 2 diabetes. I was put on a fairly strict diet, losing three stone in three months. Next on the list was a sigmoidoscopy to find out what is causing my bum problem, but everything was fine.

The next project on the medical front was a barium enema and an X-ray. They were really doing their best to get to the bottom of things. They decided I needed to go in for an op to chop something out of my bum, not piles. I was definitely not in the mood to be going into hospital again, but I thought anything to get rid of the pain at last.

Despite the pains my body seemed to be putting me through, I was determined not to become depressed. I continued to walk the fells. I found I could numb the sensations of the razor blades up my bum after half a mile of painful plodding. That summer was also good for lots of swims in several tarns around the Lakes, including twelve dips in my favourite, Beacon Tarn, near Coniston Water. I also carried out many evening walks to visit tarns for quiet swims.

As I meditated in my stone room, lots of beautiful thoughts came bubbling up from deep within me. I was saying to myself all the time how lucky I was to have met Stephen and how my obsession with loving him has created much of my happiness and love for life.

## Love in the mountains

On August 27, with the weather forecasting a dry and hot day, my dog, Boady and I were up very early and off to Buttermere. I climbed the very steep path to Bleaberry tarn for a refreshing dip, then on up to Red Pike. As I gazed along the ridge to High Stile and beyond I was struck with the beauty of the place. I had one of my spiritually meditative moments looking at the sunbeams on top of High Stile. I proceeded in a likewise manner down over High Crag and beyond. Sitting on a pinnacle on the side of Haystacks, I meditated on my happiness; for once Boady must have sensed my peacefulness and didn't whine at me to get walking.

On the way down I found a deep clear pool under a waterfall in Warnscale Beck, and did my three plunge routine. This was how I manage to swim in very cold water.

When I enter the water for the first time it is always cold, so cold. I would jump out for a few seconds, then think it wasn't so bad and go back in again, still too cold, jump out, and then, going in for the third time, I could sit in the water for ages. Cold clean clear, beautiful. I love my life, I love lots of people, love my dog but I love Stephen the most, and always will do. I must remember these lovely moments as sometimes I forget how beautiful life can be.

On 24th October, I had another quite superlative afternoon walk up Arthur's Pike above Ullswater, then on to the top of Wether Hill. There wasn't a cloud in the sky. Completely quiet, not a soul about anywhere, I shouted out, at the top of my voice, my love for Stephen. I think maybe I think of Stephen too much, but I can't help it. He is stuck in my memory. I loved him then, and I still love him now, I am totally odd I know, but who cares? I am the way that I am. Born weird. Nothing can change it, nor did I want it any way different. I loved being in love. I should have been wary of getting too happy though. I did not see the approaching rut.

CHAPTER TWENTY

# "What are you doing here?"

29th October 2010. I went into hospital for my bum op. In at 9 am, I woke up at 10.30am. I woke up shaking as I always do after an op. It's just the anaesthesia wearing off, and maybe lack of food for your diabetes, I'm told. I spent all day in a ward shaking, in pain, stomach aches. A terrible day, and then a nurse walking past saw me and said, "What are you doing here?" she continued, "This is a day ward, and you'll need moving to another ward for the night." I changed wards. That night in the ward was interminable; I couldn't lie down; I couldn't sit, and I couldn't settle. The phrase, 'What are you doing here?' was going around and around in my head.

"What are you doing here?" I remembered someone asking me that before. But I couldn't figure out where. Then another memory leapt into my mind. I got a flashback of lying in a bed in another hospital and someone asking me that question. I was not being asked that question about what I was doing at Furness General Hospital in Barrow, but at Lynfield Mount, the mental hospital in Bradford where I had the AT. These strange thoughts tipped me back into depression.

At home the following week, my depression got worse. My feelings of guilt over Stephen's death bubbled up again. I felt anxious, hopeless. These emotions affected my sleeping as I often woke up at around 3.00am. I even lost interest in working, sitting at home tearful. When I did fall asleep, I would dream of being in the bloody spaceship again. I thought I had learnt to live with all this, but now I couldn't get it out of my mind. I hadn't had this nightmare for a few years, so why has it come back now?

One day I felt very depressed, and Ness came and took me to the pub, which was a mistake as I ended up crying in the pub. Now I was not sleeping at all, just existing on catnaps. Endless thoughts were going round in my head about Stephen, the AT, being in the hospital, my past, my depressions.

I told my GP I was getting depressed again and she gave me a form to fill in which proved to her that I was depressed. I told her that I couldn't stand my mind's activities anymore. I told her about being on the receiving end of the electric shock aversion therapy, but I think she thought I meant ECT, (Electroconvulsive Therapy). ECT is a treatment that involves sending an electric current through the brain to trigger an epileptic seizure to relieve the symptoms of some mental health problem. She didn't have an understanding of electric shock AT. I asked her to look through my medical records and she would find out all about it. I liked my GP and she has done a lot for me and I am sure she will be a great help to me in the future but she is very young. She said she'd look into my records and asked me to come back and see her again next week.

On the same day, I had an appointment to see my diabetes nurse who was so worried about me that she phoned my GP and got her to see me again straight away. My GP forwarded me for a psychological assessment and put me on antidepressants. She says she thinks the waiting list for therapy is about two months or so. Meanwhile, she says I've got to do my best not to kill myself, but get myself up into the mountains and walk my doggy.

During my wait for an NHS psychologist, I went back to see Shirley, my counsellor from 2005. She was excellent for me then, and I hoped she would help me again. She made me look at things in a different light.

Shirley said the aversion therapy that I had had as a youngster was abusive and I would carry hidden memories of this and the flashbacks may well have been triggered by my recent hospital visit. In therapy with Shirley, I was trying to examine the aversion therapy memories which are slowly beginning to emerge. I hated these piecemeal memories which kept coming back. I'd just get one bit of my life sorted out so that I can live with it and then suddenly out of nowhere comes another group of memories which depress me again. I wished they would all come at once and then I could sort them all out at once.

I remembered the electric shocks as if they were happening now. I felt the shocks were trapped inside me. My stomach would spasm, my diaphragm tightening, and uncontrollable shaking. I couldn't understand why I felt like this when the AT that I remember hadn't, at the time, felt that bad. Shirley realised that when in therapy and talking about the AT, I became agitated and shook, my head, arms and legs, shaking, with fear as to what I was experiencing. In flashback, I remember waiting for the shocks to start knowing there was nothing I could do or say to stop it happening. Then Shirley instructed me to think of fell-walking and I calmed down.

In January I finally got to see an NHS therapist for a psychiatric assessment. She made another appointment. The following week she said my flashbacks of screwed up memory was like PTSD. Then I had the week off work because

I couldn't stand the thought of going out. I felt tearful and odd all the time, more so when I went out. So I stocked up on beer and sobbed the week away. I felt jittery all the time; life's too much. I'm getting arthritis in the whole of my right arm and neck to add to all the other pains in my left arm, ankles, knees, head, eyes, stomach, etc. I was on a real downer again; my memory was playing tricks again.

Painful memories long reconciled, jumped into my head at the same time as my short-term memory seems to have gone completely. It was pissing me off; making me angry. I didn't know what was going on. I thought I was going mad. I was again diagnosed with post-traumatic stress disorder. Partly concerning the AT and partly concerning the death of Stephen. I had dealt with the trauma surrounding Stephen's death and can live with that. He is in my thoughts always but now always in a positive, loving light.

Now I had to go through many very painful sessions with my therapists to try to understand what went on and why it has traumatised me so much. This seems to be by trying to make me re-live and remember what happened. I got very emotional and I used the name Carmel as a safe word, which I had to utter if the thoughts got too much and I started to breakdown. They brought me back by making me think nice thoughts and trying to stop me shaking and crying

> *I am walking down a corridor to a room where something awful will happen. I am shit scared, but I can't do anything about it. I know something is going to happen but when I reach the door and go in I get an extreme desire to escape, and a shutter comes down on my past.*

Was this a memory of my first day of electric shock therapy? I know I was scared then but not as bad as this felt. I couldn't stop getting very emotional about Stephen's death even though I have had loads of psychological help to try to get over this trauma. I know he is dead, I know he is gone, it wasn't his fault and I also know it wasn't my fault either, it was an accident. I thought I'd got over all this but I have a recurring memory of this traumatic event in my head that won't go away.

> *It was the night, it wasn't the night, it was the dark, I am afraid of the dark, in the dark bad things happen, I have just had another flashback of being in the dark and being absolutely terrified of something that was about to happen, but then my mental memory block drops down and I can't see, I can't get through it.*

## Progress

By mid-February, I believed I was making progress with both my therapists and I was quite happy about it. Some may say I was being unethical in having two therapists at the same time, but from my point of view, I was receiving two different methods.

The NHS therapist had her method called Cognitive Behavioural Therapy (CBT). She doesn't want to go near my AT memories and wants to deal with me in the here and now, trying to change my way of looking at the past thus changing the way I behave. She is leading me through the process. Creating a timeline as to what happened when. We were time constrained to one hour and no longer. This was similar to the type of psychotherapy I received in 1999. But I was sceptical of this approach as it didn't solve my problems before and I needed to get something sorted out this time.

With Shirley, there was a lot more delving into my memories and trying to understand and remember what went on, in particular, the meanings of my nightmares.

There were less structure and more time, as long as I needed, sometimes up to two or three hours, and she always grounds me before I leave. Different therapists, different methods, different results but definite positive progress. But perhaps not.

> *I remembered waking up in bed, "What are you doing here?" asked a nurse but I couldn't remember my name, couldn't work out where I was, totally shit scared, afraid, a frightening experience, I remembered seeing Stephen die and I broke down in tears.*

CHAPTER TWENTY ONE

# ESCAPE!

One of my problems at this time was a lack of sleep. It was not just not being able to sleep per se, it was more to do with being afraid to go to sleep at all. That's where the bad dreams were. If I do fall asleep, I wake up after a couple of hours with my diaphragm tightening in spasms. Something is stuck in my throat. I swallow repeatedly, but it doesn't clear. Then what follows is a world of negativities going around in my head. Little things throw me into a panic. Blaming myself for everything that went wrong.

Where's my phone? Chucking everything about madly looking for it. I know, I'll ring myself up on my landline, then I'll hear the ringing tone, but damn it, I can't remember my number. I've lost my keys. I lost count of the number of things I lost. I had to leave messages on my mobile phone to remember things. Then I'd forget that I did that. I said to people my memory is like a sieve. Not a normal sieve. One with the mesh bit missing, so anything dropped in it went straight through and disappeared into the abyss.

In frustration I'd go into my meditation room, light some incense, wrap myself up in my pentagram rug and try to stop the shaking. I would strive to slow my breathing down until I could relax the tensions within my body and put my mind at rest. I actually managed to fall asleep rolled up in my rug sometimes, getting through till morning, and waking up to find my black-haired friend was keeping me company. The nightmares were waiting for me when I fell asleep, almost exclusively the spaceship one, but also one where I am in the midst of a load of black balloons which I am constantly trying to climb up through but never getting anywhere.

Some nights, rather than go to bed where I knew I wouldn't sleep, I'd lie on my big leather recliner in front of my TV and channel surf until it was a suitable time to get up as normal people do. I wandered around my house in a daze. How come they say memories come back when you are ready to deal with them? I was plainly not ready for all this.

I'd hoped that my last major depression of five years ago was my last. I thought I'd suffered enough. I just wanted to be at peace. Why wouldn't my past leave me alone? But no, just more pain with things past coming back to haunt me. How can I shut my mind down? I tried my best to meditate and play soothing music which worked for a while.

The weather was so bad that I couldn't even get out into the mountains either. Well I could, but there's no pleasure in getting cold and wet.

> *I got in my spaceship again last night. I woke up screaming and swearing "Oh fuck, what the fuck is happening to me?" I am afraid, my aches and pains feel worse, the uncontrollable shaking and trembling, I can't calm down, there are some awful memories coming back and I'm frightened. I am at the mercy of my past haunting me. I am losing control.*

**Saved by a friend**

I didn't realise just how important Boady, my little doggy, was for me until all these flashbacks and panic attacks started. I was sprawled out on my chair one morning trying not to think of anything, she pounced onto my lap. She often did this when she wanted something. It would be food, it was always food. That's why her nickname was Piggyboad. After I had shoved her down, I filled her bowl with biscuits. As the bowl rapidly emptied, I said to her "Okay, Piggyboad, do you want to go out for a walk?" She glanced up at me, sending me a look that said. "Sure Dad, just got to empty my bowl first."

I drove down to the beach to her favourite place. This is where a long spit of flat sand lay amongst the otherwise pebble strewn beach. Here we would play rollystones. I would fill all my pockets with golf-ball sized pebbles, Boady bounced around me in circles, barking madly as she knew what was coming next. I would roll one pebble at high speed along the sand and she runs off after it until it stops, she doesn't pick it up though, she turns and runs at high speed back towards me and as she passes me I roll a pebble in the direction she is running. As I roll the stones back and forth, my daft pooch chases them, barking her head off.

This game goes on until I have just one pebble left for the special place. At the end of the tongue of sand it runs down into the sea, well not really the sea, it is the River Leven as it makes its way out into the estuary. There is always water here no matter what the tide is doing. She always follows this last pebble until she disappears into the water with a big spladooosh, funny pooch.

Having Boady close by when I was having a flashback leading into a panic attack meant I had a means of escape. I'd sit down on the floor with her sprawled out between my legs. Then I would start to brush her hair. At some point, she'd roll over for a belly rub and with her help I would slowly drag myself back to reality.

*I am building a tower. Out of blocks. The bottom block has a locked door in it. Behind the door there is a key. As I build the tower I know that if I finish it, the door will open automatically and I can retrieve the key. As I reach up and put the last block on, I hear the door open below me, I climb back down and as I make my way to the open door something comes out from behind me and smashes into the tower, which comes tumbling down and as it falls the door shuts itself. I have to start again. I know the key is important but I don't know why.*

I have a memory blockage which I am trying to break through. I thought it might be the door to the hospital therapy room. During sessions with Shirley, she suggested I try to visualise the door, change its appearance, smell, taste, sight. When I have the door in my mind she suggests I go open the door. This I manage to do but immediately I enter the room, I get an absolutely massive feeling of dread and fear. I had to get out of that room. I suddenly got an overwhelming sense of the word "ESCAPE!" in my head and I broke down.

"Perhaps you did escape," said Shirley. She reckons that with me tied down I had no physical means of escape. My body couldn't escape but my mind could. She reckons I may have done something called Dissociation.

Shirley has told me that I must try my best not to go near my memory block, as she thinks I wouldn't be able to handle it on my own. She said my best coping mechanism is to remind myself that I am lucky to have met and fallen in love with the most beautiful boy in the world; to remember I have him forever in my heart, which makes me feel so good and always calms me down when I am stressed. Another good memory was for me to imagine I am building one of my stonewalls in the Lakeland fells, trying to break the link to whatever is frightening me.

It was taking me progressively longer to calm down now when I remembered anything. Maybe I shouldn't go there at all, but my past seems to be re-emerging at unpredictable times. I was scared that I will be out in town when I had an episode. Once I was out walking Boady on the beach when I started off on one. I started shaking and crying, collapsing on the pebbles. It was a good thing no-one was about.

CHAPTER TWENTY TWO

# "I have just had an awful thought."

**In therapy with Shirley on 3rd March 2011.**

We had been going through traumatic episodes for a few days when I suddenly managed to get past the shutter that always came down when I tried to remember my time in the shock room.

I am lying naked on a bed, electrodes attached to my right forearm as usual. Both my wrists are attached to the sides of the bed. The doctor is talking to me. Not the usual doctor. Doctor Grumpy. My head is shaking with fear. Grumpy kept asking about Stephen:

"Can you think of Stephen?"

*What a stupid question I thought, I never stop thinking about him.*

"Are you thinking about him?"

Knowing what's coming, I tense up and say, "Yes."

*Immediately I get a 'zap' as the shock runs up my arm into my neck.*

"What are you doing with Stephen?" "Talking."

"Are you naked with Stephen?" "No."

"I want you to imagine you are naked with Stephen."

"Are you with him?"

*I don't want to answer him, but I know I have to. If I don't, the shock comes anyway. At least if I answer I can take in a big gulp of air and prepare my body for the pain..*

"Yes."

*Zap, this time I feel the electric shock shoot into my body and I feel my diaphragm spasm.*

"You know you have a terrible disease? We are trying to help you, Jeremy."

"You know what God says about being a homosexual?"

*It went quiet for a minute and then his voice started again, but it sounded odd.*

"You must imagine being with Stephen."

"Are you with him." "Yes."

*Zap, the shocks were getting stronger, but so was my desire to keep my love for Stephen.*

"Do you think Stephen wants you?"

"He doesn't love you, Jeremy, he has rejected you, he goes out with girls"

"He doesn't want you, he hates you."

"He doesn't hate me."

*Even my own voice sounded odd, far away. But I hadn't said anything, was I dreaming again?*

"You must get Stephen out of your head."

"Why do you still love him, Jeremy? He's left you."

"Do you love Stephen?"

"Yes." Zap, another fucking shock, but I hadn't said anything.

*I couldn't figure out what was going on, then it snapped, it was a tape recording. I was listening to my own voice.*

"We won't stop until you stop loving Stephen, this will be your salvation."

"Don't you want to please your parents?"

"You have to forget about Stephen, kill off all your thoughts about Stephen."

"Is your love for Stephen dead yet?"

"No." Zap, more pain.

*I thought to myself whatever you do to me, I will never stop loving Stephen.*

The tape clicks off and I hear him say, "It's your disease that is making you think this."

"Don't you want to be cured of your disease?"

"Yes. No. I don't know."

"There is something wrong with you and we are just trying to make you better."

*How can I stop the pain? I want it to stop. So I lied.*

"Okay, I don't love him any more."

"That's good Jeremy, I want you to tell me again, you hate him now don't you?"

*How can I answer? I betrayed him once, but never again.*

"No I don't hate him, he never did me any harm, why should I hate him?"

"You still love him then?"

There was a click, back to the recording,

"Do you love Stephen?" "Yes."

*Zap. . . I feel pain. All I feel now is pain. No not just pain, I feel love for Stephen.*

"He doesn't love you, Jeremy, he has rejected you, he goes out with girls"

"He doesn't want you, he hates you."

> *I love him so much. I know our relationship is over. I know I haven't seen him for ages. I do not want to lose my love for him. Why are they punishing me for loving him?*
>
> *I wanted to escape the pain but I didn't know how.*

At some point during these thoughts as I repeated them out loud to Shirley, I got a really odd feeling in my head that ... ?

Shirley was looking at me,

I said to her, "I have just had an awful thought."

I go quiet. I can't make sense of what I am feeling. There are all sorts of jumbled memories going around in my head; waiting for Stephen; watching him cross the road; watching him slip in the snow; get up again; brushing the snow off his trousers and walk towards me.

"What was it?"

"No, it's too much."

"Tell me what you thought."

"Maybe Stephen isn't dead, maybe these images aren't right. I don't know, I don't know what I mean. This is all a nightmare."

In a state of extreme duress, with no physical means of escape, my brain had taken it upon itself to protect me from further pain by making up some form of memory out of a jumble of true memories adding them up to make a whole false one.

I have no idea whether these false memories came to me when I was awake or asleep, all I do remember is waking up in the mental hospital with these images in my head. I totally accepted it as true.

Shirley thinks that maybe they went too far with the electric shocks and I had a breakdown.

She thinks that I may have been kept in the hospital overnight, leading a nurse to ask what I was doing there.

CHAPTER TWENTY THREE

# Panic attacks

## Finding Stephen

My response to these memories was to collapse into a near catatonic state. I couldn't move. This can't be right. I saw him die. I saw it. It happened. In trying to make sense of it, I was doubting my own memory. It was such a strong memory, everything that happened around it. How can it be untrue? I was totally confused. These thoughts were running around and around in my mind.

Then, a different thought flashed through my mind. If I didn't see Stephen die then he must be alive somewhere. I told Shirley, but she quickly brought me back to reality when she said, "what you are seeing now, Jeremy, may be wrong, he may still have died in that accident." But I was determined to find out.

That evening I went online, to find out where I could search for people past and present. I had to pay loads of money for credits but that was nothing in my quest to find Stephen. By checking deaths for the period before Xmas in 1972, I found that he didn't die when I thought he did. This proved that my vision of him dying was false.

I was elated, and I needed to tell someone. I contacted two of my best friends, Vickie and Malcolm to tell them what I had found out. Malcolm said, "He might be married with loads of kids and has completely forgotten you." I said, "I don't care, I just want to see him."

Online I looked for Stephen, now being very glad he told me his middle name which he so disliked but was extremely rare. I couldn't find his name anywhere. I thought maybe he had gone abroad. Being a linguist he could have gone anywhere. I wondered how I would find him if he had. Then I noticed that there were two death records for his initials from the 80's so I clicked on to see who they were. There he was. The record said he died in March 1984.

## A Month of Panic

I felt totally numb, in pain again, tears, crying, my Stephen is dead. I saw him die, but I didn't. He was dead then he wasn't. He was alive and now he is dead again. I was so depressed now that I needed a reason not to kill myself there and then. Luckily I heard the gentle thump of a wagging tail as I was brought back to reality.

Some may think that finding out the truth about Stephen meant I was free from my depression but that was not the case. My panic attacks got worse. I felt uncontrollable fear, shaking, feeling I was going mad. My release was to dissociate to the good memories of being with Stephen. As always with me, always looking for reasons to blame myself for anything that goes wrong. I needed to find the reason I was forced to come up with seeing Stephen die. I had virtually killed him. Why had my younger self, Jeremy, believed it so completely? I couldn't understand it.

I was subjected to countless panic attacks over the next six months. They started with me remembering something or having a flashback of the electric shocks. My head would begin to shake, which would make my neck follow suit, losing control. Then a horrible feeling, thinking I am going to choke, swallowing endlessly to try and get rid of a blockage in my throat. I had no sense of time when an attack came.

When I came down from one I knew it would be just a matter of time before the next one hit. I would start shaking uncontrollably. This lasted for hours and sometimes all day, with pain in my shoulder, the itching forearm, shaking legs and hands. I sought relief by dissociating.

One day when I did find the strength to go to work, I was sat, quiet in my thoughts, when Ness asked, "How long did the AT go on for?"

"Six months or so," I said.

"Well why did you keep going?" she said, "How could you return home or to school after treatment? Why didn't you stop going?"

"I couldn't stop going, I was scared of being expelled. I was ashamed of what I was."

I needed to be alone in my agony. I couldn't let anyone know that I was going mad. One Sunday morning, I awoke at 2am to a pulsating pain just over my right eye. It felt like a sharp knife was piercing my forehead. The panic attack then developed into the throat problem, chest tightening and the shakes. I tried to eat something to force whatever was in my throat down but I couldn't eat or drink.

Feeling increasingly anxious, I phoned NHS Direct for help. They told me to go to see a doctor at Furness General Hospital in Barrow. When I asked how I was supposed to drive there feeling like I did, I was told "If you can't drive you should either get a taxi or wait till morning and get a bus." I should have told them I was having a heart attack or something.

I went and sat in my Landrover and tried to stop shaking. It took a while to calm down enough to drive the thirty minutes to Barrow. I noticed that when I actually started driving, being more in control, my madness settled down.

It was about 3am when I got to hospital. As I was sitting in the cold, surprisingly empty waiting room, I managed to keep calm by breathing deeply. When I first saw the male doctor, I felt anxious again. I think I have an underlying fear of men in white coats. How was I supposed to tell this man who I had never met before about my problem?

The shaking got worse as I tried to tell this chap why I was there. He took some persuading but did give me a number of 5mg diazepam. I think I really wanted sleeping pills but he wouldn't prescribe them. He asked if I had driven to the hospital, when I said I had, he said that I shouldn't take the diazepam straight away, I should drive home before I do so. I drove home as fast as I could, went inside and downed four of them straight away.

Later that day, I got an appointment with my GP at 3.30pm. I got there on time as usual but unknown to me, the booking-in system was down and I didn't get seen till 5.40. The long wait made me feel jittery and I got the shakes in waiting room. I had to sit at the back, avoiding people's stares. Eventually I got more diazepam.

Despite taking diazepam to help me sleep, I woke up in panic attack mode again, seeing Stephen die, but now I know he didn't. I shouted out aloud at the top of my voice in frustration. What is fantasy? What is true and false? I went to work on my own, I needed to be on my own for the day.

I drove to Sedbergh to do a site visit and forced myself to talk to a farmer. I am okay, I am good at my job. I am in control. I know what I am doing. I visited Charlotte on the way home for a chat. I didn't make my decision to visit her until the last moment. I am glad I did, we had a good natter, and she had bad news. She'd been made redundant from her job after twenty-five years. I told her I was depressed too, so we sat together and tried to cheer each other up.

One evening at home, alone, I felt an overwhelming feeling of sadness. I can think positive for a while then I get another reminder of past traumatic memories. I saw Stephen die again, even though I know it didn't happen, feel tired, sad, can't get it out of my head. Tired and crying I bought a load of beer, a bottle of Scotch and drank myself into oblivion.

I woke up thinking of Stephen, extreme pain in my right shoulder, and along my forearm. Electric shock memories, people talking to me. Sat at the side of my bed, extreme body shakes pains in arms, short of breath, I stood up and fell over, stomach ache, head shaking, not an AT memory just crying with grief and loss for Stephen.

I walked down to the beach with Boady, the tide was out so I could walk far out into Morecambe Bay where I shouted, "AAAAAAARGH" a few times as loud as I could. I am obsessed with Stephen, confusion in my head, on the one hand people are telling me to move on from him, but on the other I can't let him go. He brought me so much, I don't want anyone else, just need people to understand me and let me do my own thing.

I was left with so many questions. What happened to Stephen? And how did he actually die? Was he subjected to AT? What had he thought when I never contacted him again? Why didn't he contact me? Was he warned off me? How come since he was alive we never bumped into each other in Bradford?

After leaving the mental health hospital in 1972, I came out with a vision and belief that I saw Stephen die. Where did those thoughts come from? Brainwashing? Power of suggestion? I was brought up to believe that everything that went wrong was my fault, I never did anything right. It must have been me who thought of it, to escape the pain of AT- why didn't I just come out of the mental hospital and know the truth? And carry on with life. Look up Stephen. Why did I come out so totally convinced that Stephen was dead? So convinced that I never looked for him? That vision and belief was in my head for nearly forty years before I questioned it.

Why now? Why hadn't I questioned it before?

I found out later that I had, from my therapy notes in 1999. But no-one had picked up on it.

CHAPTER TWENTY FOUR

# The diary of shame

My parents had been getting along as old people do. They had down-sized from our big old family house to a flat in sheltered housing. They had to throw loads of stuff out. In among everything a box of my mum's diaries was found and I asked to see them. I suppose it might be considered as being a bit naughty reading my mum's diaries but I couldn't resist; anyway I was just getting my own back for when she read mine. I went straight to the diary for 1972 to see if she mentioned anything.

Here is the list of entries concerning me from her 1972 diary.

Sat 8th April Jeremy Leeds night out

*I was with Stephen, this is when I realised our relationship would soon be over.*

Wed 12th April Jeremy back to school

*My breakdown at school probably happened the following week. One month or thereabouts I had to go through priests brainwashing me to convince me that I had an awful disease.*

Sun 14th May Jeremy refusing to go to mass

Mon 15th May Jeremy gone to see GP

Wed 24th May St Bedes meeting about Jeremy...awful day

Wed 31st May School again about Jeremy

Thurs 1st June Jeremy psy (Bfd) 9:30

*This is the day I was first taken up to the mental hospital to see the psychiatrist.*

Mon 5th June Had to phone school about Jeremy J (A)

Tues 6 June Jeremy psy (Bfd) J (A)

Wed 7th June J (A)

Thurs 8th June J (A)

Fri 9th June J psy (Bfd) J (A)

Tues 13th June J (A)

Wed 14th June Jeremy psy (Bfd) J (A)

Thurs 15th June Jeremy psy (Bfd) 10 am

Mon 19th June Jeremy psy (Bfd) 10.30

Wed 21st June Jeremy psy (Bfd) 11.15

Wed 28th June Jeremy psy (Bfd)

Tues 15th Aug Jeremy failed all his A levels.

Sat 2nd Sept Ring St Bedes about Jeremy.

Fri 6th Oct Meeting St Bedes about Jeremy

Wed 29th Nov Went to hospital to see Jeremy

*Apparently I was in hospital. It doesn't say why. I can't remember it.*

The mentions above of J (A) are the days I sat my A level exams. As you can see I was being treated with AT on the same day as I sat three of my exams. It appears to me that my parents knew all about my visits to the loony bin and had discussions about me with the school.

There are countless 'DG's throughout her diaries and for a while it had me stumped until on one occasion she wrote Deo Gratias (Thank God). She was forever thanking her God for everything. There are times when a son passes something and then it has DG following it. At no point does it say "Well done son" or anything like that. There is one day in 1975 where she says of me, 'Jeremy bad again.' There is no mention in any of her diaries that mention anything about me being gay.

I had been told by the Headmaster not to tell my parents and I never did. Yet when my brother asked them in 1999 if they knew about it, they denied all knowledge. I wondered if somewhere in the Catholic religion it says that while it is 'normally' a sin to tell lies, telling lies to an abnormal, diseased, homosexual son was okay.

I am beginning to think my parents were brainwashed by the Catholic priests at school into believing that the best way to deal with their queer son was to endlessly tell him that God was good and deny all knowledge of anything else.

I rang my brother, Neil, to tell him that my parents knew what happened to me and he was shocked to learn that they had lied to us that day when he asked them if they knew anything about it. There was obviously nothing I can do about this new information, they being far too old and senile to confront them with any of this.

They both died in 2015. I went to my mum's funeral, but I did not enter the church. When I last saw my dad it was at the reception after her funeral. When my gaze met his, I could still see the same look that he had always given me ever since I had come out to him over forty years before. I didn't go to his funeral.

It really pissed me off to learn that it was more important for my parents to eradicate my homosexuality than it was for me to pass my A levels and go to university. I have no doubt they were convinced by my school that they had to get on with it, but they could have waited until I had taken my exams.

I believe that it didn't matter to them, if I failed my A levels. The last thing they wanted at that time was for me to get away to university, where they would have had no hold about how I lived my life. They needed to keep me close so that they could cure me. Maybe this explained too, why my dad had charged me so little rent money. It must have really upset him that he had to forgo some money just so they could keep their eyes on me.

## CHAPTER TWENTY FIVE

# Defragging my memories

My need for therapy continued and very slowly, I began to sort things out in my head. I had many sessions with Shirley regarding PTSD, dissociation, body memories, implicit memories and explicit memories. The frequent panic attacks continued but slowly reduced to two or three a week.

It is obvious to me now, that all the bits of memories over the years relating to the aversion therapy have been fragmentary due to the trauma of it all. My brain hid most of this period behind a very thick wall. Shirley told me that if I could turn my implicit memories into a form of narrative, then I will have changed them into explicit memories. Therefore to understand my past I ought to talk and write about it.

I've tried to turn my traumatic memories into a story. Using the theory that if I could explain my story to other people, then I would be able to understand it myself. I began contacting all my friends, ringing them up, or visiting them and trying to explain it to them. I have got to thank all of them, especially Vickie, Charlotte, Andrew, Lou, Shaun and Sam, Malcolm, Janet, Eileen, Julie and Jim.

### The story of late 1972

One day on my way to the hospital for my weekly dose of torture, I'd already decided that when I got to the end of

Leylands Lane, instead of going straight across the road and up Duchy Drive to the Hospital, I would turn right and go to the pub. The Hare and Hounds. I often sat in this pub, drinking on my own when I was supposed to be at school. I took my schoolbag with me as I wasn't intending to go back to school that day.

After a few pints, I decided to go and see if Stephen was at home. I had never been to his house, but knew his address. After wandering around a bit, I found his house on a cul de sac. I approached the door with some trepidation, but the beer had convinced me that I was doing the right thing. I knocked at the door and his dad answered. I'd only ever seen his dad a couple of times at school, at those parent/teacher meetings, but I'd never talked to him before. Nervously I asked if Stephen was in?

He just said, "No, Stephen isn't here, he is away." I asked him if he had an address for him, but his dad just said. "No, we are not sure where he is." I thought that was a bit odd but I couldn't do anything about it, and sloped off, not sure what I was going to do.

I thought I'd find another pub somewhere and as I stumbled along Allerton Road in the direction of the city centre, a car pulled up next to me. Someone got out but I wasn't paying attention. I heard a shout, "Is that you, Gavins?" I turned to see the priest I had initially confessed my homosexuality to, standing by the car. I was shocked and realised Stephen's dad must have reported me to the school. The priest said,

"You are a disappointment to us, Jeremy. We thought you were doing well with your treatment, but obviously you are not trying hard enough. We will take you for your appointment now."

I got into the back seat of the car. The driver was another teacher.

On the way back to the loony bin, the priest told me that I was stupid for trying to see Stephen as he didn't want to have anything to do with me. I must go for more treatment because while I still wanted to be with Stephen, I was obviously not cured.

"We can still cure you but you will have to co-operate, and don't forget, we can still expel you if you don't."

I had been a stupid idiot trying to see Stephen. When we reached the hospital, I got out of the car clutching my schoolbag.

I was taken in once more to see Grumpy, the head doctor. He told me that they would continue the treatment. I thought, *Oh well more of the same, maybe I ought to try and convince them somehow that the treatment is working.*

He then interrogated me again but this time it was all about me and Stephen; why I wanted to see him; what I thought of him. He wanted to know what we did together sexually. He seemed to be greatly interested in the kinds of sex we had and asked me all sorts of questions about it. The doctor then told me to go home, saying,

"It's too late to have a session today, but make sure you come back next week."

The following week I made my way back to the changing room, stripped and changed into a dressing gown and once more flip-flopped my way down the corridor. I knocked and waited, "Come in." I entered the room and, taking my gown off, went across to the chair and sat down, waiting for the doctor to strap me in.

It wasn't until I sat down, that I noticed that there were no screens to look at. There was a hospital trolley bed. I was surprised to see Dr Grumpy. I'd never seen him in here before. He told me to get up and lie face up on the bed. He tied my arms to each side of the bed, then attached the electrodes to my right forearm. I noticed that he had forgotten to give me the left hand switch which stopped the shocks. When I pointed this out, he said, "You won't need it."

I was getting frightened now, because even though I had been coming here for many months, this was the first time anything had changed. I'd got used to the younger doctor. This doctor's gruff disinterested attitude was far more threatening. I wondered if it was part of the job description for these psychiatrists, to be as objectionable as possible.

### The shocks begin again

Dr Grumpy had taped my conversations of me talking about Stephen and what we did together. He played them back to me, giving me shocks at regular intervals. He told me I was diseased. The recording told me I was sick. I was in a state of terrible confusion, in love with Stephen but having to go through the ordeal of being physically punished for saying it. I tried lying but then he just played the tape again and there was no escape.

I have no idea how long this went on for, nor do I remember whether I stayed there or went home each day. The answer to those questions are still hidden deep in my mind. I tried to resist but I couldn't. I tried to keep my love for Stephen intact, but it got more difficult to do. I had to find a way of shielding my love for Stephen from the pains of the electric shocks, but found it increasingly hard to stay in control.

I'd just about got used to the picture show treatment but this was far harder to take. In the earlier treatment I had some control over my thoughts and feelings but now I had completely lost control. No wonder I have always disliked hearing the sound of my own voice.

## Trying to make sense of these memories

This was completely different to the other therapy where I was shown pictures. Here it was my imagination they were working on. Shaming me and making me anxious when I thought of Stephen, telling me he hates me and has forgotten me, doesn't want to see me anymore. I couldn't believe this and was sinking into a morass of confusion.

Sometimes my coping mechanism when the flashback panic tremors start, is to dissociate to being with Stephen and my love for him calms me down. So every time I think of him I am at peace, but every time the shock trauma appears I am in meltdown, so must this not mean that when the shocks started, I dissociated to being with Stephen as an image to cut out the pain? When he wasn't in my mind, when I was not dissociating, then the pain would return.

When I was told to imagine him and I did and then they shocked me, I must have found a way to shield out the thoughts of Stephen from the pain I was receiving, because otherwise when I thought of Stephen, I would have no relief from the pain. If this confuses you then it completely baffles me. I must have split my mind from my body in a bid to escape, but that was a very scary place. I was flitting back and forth between reality and unreality.

CHAPTER TWENTY SIX

# Fighting the flashbacks

In July I had my last session with my Cognitive Behavioural Therapist. We had made quite good progress over the last four months. Stephen was dead, not dead, and definitely dead. I really do have to try and find some positives out of this. I wanted to go back to feeling like I did in October 2010, when I was up in the mountains shouting out my joy for having known him. All the years of hating and blaming my younger self have got to stop. I have to thank myself for finding the strength to keep going all through those decades of depression.

One good thing is that I have found some form of happiness on my own, single and free. I must admit it would be nice for me to have a relationship with a physically close nature to it. I am not sure that I am capable of that though, I have been a recluse sexually for so long now, I know no other way of life.

## Backpacking

I decided to return to something I used to enjoy in my twenties. I had walked many miles, backpacking around Wales, The Lakes and Northern Scotland, and I was determined to start again. A bit old at fifty-seven, but it would give me an excuse to keep fit. Over the next few weeks, I accumulated new backpacking gear. I bought a one man and a dog tent, sleeping bag, cook set, waterproofs, rucksack and clothes. All told it came to over £1,500 but more importantly my whole pack, without food and liquid, weighed about twelve pounds.

On the 17th August 2011, my dog and I set off from home towards the Lakes with Allen Crags as my prime objective. Allen Crags is the first mountain in the alphabetical list of Wainright's Lakeland fells. Using my extensive knowledge of the Lakes, I had some idea of where I would camp each night. After about twelve miles we arrived at our first campsite, above Torver. A lovely patch of flat turf next to a stream, perfect. Dangling my feet in the cold stream, I ate my pesto, pasta and tinned skippers. I had fun trying to entice Boady into the tent. She did get the idea eventually, and then over the next three nights she took to sleeping at the bottom of my tent, which was a bit of a pain as there was plenty of room beside me. That first night I fell asleep lying half out of the tent, looking up at the stars.

The second day found us walking over Walna Scar into the Duddon Valley and along the riverside path to a campsite at the bottom of Ore gap below Bowfell. No stargazing as the clouds had rolled in with the rain forcing me into the tent for a long night. Boady loved being in water but didn't much like the rain, so came into the tent with no problems. It was lovely to hear her gentle snoring, hopefully she thought the same about my far louder version.

It felt good to be on a walk where I could just go where I wanted, without having to return to the starting point, like ordinary day walking. On the third day, the weather deteriorated as I plodded along, and Boady found even more puddles to sit in. Making my way up past Bowfell we entered the clouds and rain. On the top of Allen Crags, I missed the view as I viewed the mist.

I had taken a pedometer with me so I could log my mileage. It was just over twenty-five miles from home to the top of Allen Crags, and 6340 feet of ascent. Then we were off again down past Angle Tarn and then bee-lining across the hills, mostly off paths, to camp at Codale tarn for a very wet stormy night. Boady's insistence that she slept at the bottom of the tent, thereby rubbing against the tent wall, meant we both got wet. A happy dog can be a right pain as it wags its tail against the tent wall.

The last day was a pleasant dry sunny seven mile walk around Helm Crag to the Traveller's Rest at Grasmere, where I met Charlotte for a well earned beer and a lift home. Thirty-eight miles walked over four days. Apart from shoulder pains at night and the cold showery weather for the most part, we had a great time. I didn't think about my depressions at all. I did think about Stephen a lot but that's just the way I am. I felt satisfactorily tired.

I couldn't wait to get going again on our next trip. I could probably cut my pack size down and still have enough stuff, so the going would be easier. It would have helped if I managed to find a way for Boady to carry her own food, but since she liked to dive into every pool of water she found, or roll around in muddy peat, it would never have worked. Life was turning good again, then it got even better.

### The itch finally releases its grip on my fore-arm

16th September, I woke up suddenly at 4.30 with my usual pain in my shoulder; with a panic attack on the way. Thinking I was going mad again. The sharp knife piercing into my right eyebrow. I now had two pains going on, and the itch in my arm came back with a suddenness that really hurt.

I had a terrifying flashback of lying on a bed and being given electric shocks as someone was trying to get me to answer his questions. I wanted to rip the electrodes off my arm but I couldn't and I had to accept the biting pain. I remember as I waited for the next shock to go through me I tensed my shoulder knowing I would soon be in pain.

Suddenly, instead of trying to fight the onset of more misery, I thought "*maybe my body is trying to talk to me, to get my attention*" and, just as suddenly as they came, the pains left me and I felt an overwhelming surge of peace spread through me. I still felt like I was going mad again, but then I thought maybe I am not, "*maybe it is my body trying to tell me something and for a change I ought to listen.*"

My mind was always pushing my body away, leaving it behind when I dissociated. This may account for the countless injuries I have had, my body repeatedly trying to wake my mind to the injustices and false memories which were in my head. Or there again it may explain why I have had so many injuries in the first place, while my mind is off on 'a dissociation event.'

A dissociation event is how I describe something that has just happened that in its own context doesn't make any sense at all, unless it was to be recognised as a time when my mind has not been associated with my body. My body was left to fend for itself which it fails to do and then I have an accident.

Over the years of rock-climbing, playing rugby and general bum problems, I have had repeated visits to hospitals for operations. I have always awoken from these operations in a bed shaking and frightened. The nurses forever telling me that it was the anaesthesia wearing off, but now I know it wasn't.

The awakening after the operation in October 2010, finally broke through a barrier into my subconciousness to reveal a forgotten true memory to me. I believe now that my body had been attempting this for many years.

I now know why I get strange pains around my body. It is the body memories of the electroshocks, of where they attached the electrodes to forearm, and my body tensing up every time I knew a shock was coming. At last I knew what all those unexplained pains were. With this knowledge my arm stopped itching. The itch had finally served its purpose, to act as a physical reminder of locked-away hidden memories.

My forearm hasn't itched since.

## Changing the storyline of a false memory

I'd come a long way in the few months since I felt that my vision of Stephen's death was false. I had great trouble in sorting out my feelings about this. I was just as depressed and continued to have flashbacks, this time more about the AT than Stephen. Since I had an in-built compulsion to blame myself for whatever went wrong in my life, I now blamed myself for having had this false memory. I was responsible for Stephens's death memory in that I imagined it happening. I believed it. I thought I was keeping Stephen's memory alive for all these years when some of the time he was not even dead. I was totally confused by it all. I couldn't get my head round it. I couldn't get the memory of his death out of my head. I was seeking reasons to blame myself for thinking up such a memory, what must have happened to me to make me kill him?

One morning I woke up in pain, and trying to control it, thinking I must accept the pain to protect Stephen. My mind and body battling each other for control, then the bad stomach shocks began and a piercing pain above my right eye, shakes, all these are body memories of the traumatic AT. I was still getting the memory of his death even though I now knew it didn't happen. Shirley encouraged me to script a new ending to the road accident. After much thought I came up with the following script.

Instead of him seeing me and running blindly across the road, I see the danger and shout out, "No Stephen. Stop," at the top of my voice; he hears me, stops, and the vehicle goes past. He is looking at me from the middle of the road; I run out and grab him, pull him to safety, hug him and whisper in his ear:

"That was a silly thing to do, you might have been killed"

The accident that didn't happen, didn't happen because these are the sensations I had at the time based on the points of the pentagram. During meditation, I actively thought about this and succeeded in exchanging my new script for the one where Stephen died.

AIR/SOUND. Seeing the danger, I shout to him to stop. The noisy wagon goes past through the slushy snow, noise dies down. I am alert and in control of the situation.

SPIRIT/SIGHT. He is standing in the middle of the road with a look of shock on his face. Then he started smiling at me, he is alive!

EARTH/TOUCH. I run out to him, and pulled him off the road; we hugged each other; grounding ourselves after a frightening experience.

FIRE/SMELL. The beautiful aroma of his hair as I hug him. Feeling the passion running through me.

WATER/TASTE. Our lips part as we kiss; the emotions of what happened overwhelms us.

I have saved him, I am in control, and we go down the back street laughing and hugging, throwing snowballs at each other.

I remember Stephen giving me the pentagram; it has kept us connected and it always will.

## CHAPTER TWENTY SEVEN

# The boy who died twice

Despite making up my new ending to Stephen's accident, I still knew it was false. I decided I needed to do something practical to help me sort myself out. I would set about finding out all I could about what happened to Stephen. How he had lived and how he had died.

I found that I could send for Stephen's birth and death certificates. The birth certificate revealed the origin of his very distinctive middle name, Carmel, without which I would've really struggled to find him.

The death certificate said he died in Blackburn in 1983. The cause of death was given as shock, haemorrhage and multiple injuries. There was a coroners inquest in 1984, which I assume is why the family research sites I used had 1984 as the year of his death.

I rang up the Catholic Church in Bradford where Stephen lived, to see if I could find anything about where he might be buried. I talked to a priest who knew his parents well. He said though he never knew him, Stephen's parents had told him that he had died in a road accident. He was driving home after his girlfriend had dumped him and crashed on a motorway slip road. Both his parents were now dead, and since his parents were cremated, the priest thought Stephen may have been cremated too, though he didn't know where. The fact that Stephen died in a road accident made me shudder, and question whether I should continue my search, but I needed to know.

I set out to find where his ashes were buried. I rang around a few cemeteries in both Blackburn and Bradford and found him in Bradford. Using my knowledge of incense making, I made up some incense to burn to commemorate life, love and death. I also mixed a pentagram elemental oil. I drove down to Bradford on April 18, 2012 and I visited his resting place. There wasn't an exact spot but a general place where the cemetery people interned ashes for deaths occurring in October 1983.

Sitting on a nearby bench, trying to work out where his ashes might be, a blackbird swooped down and landed near me. I took the hint and laid his pentagram on the ground where the bird had landed. I burnt the incense and pentagram oil I had made especially for the visit. Then I sang the words of 'Reach Out I'll Be There' twice. Once to him as I remembered my part in his life, and again through my tears, as I remembered the time he read them to me. Then in an effort to think of him laughing, I sang our favourite bits of the song 'Come Together.'

The day after I visited Stephen's grave, I drove to my old school. I parked near the place I would have left school to walk up to the hospital. I got out of the Landrover and started to walk up the road, but I got the beginnings of another panic attack. I returned to my Landy and just sat there, hugging Boady until the shaking stopped. I couldn't go, after all these years I am scared of going there. I then drove around to where I saw Stephen die, and had no problem walking around there even though my heart was racing from the memory. I remembered meeting him here a number of times, in rain, sun and snow. I imagined him crossing the road, or me going to see him. My body had no problems going there, meaning the fear was held in my mind, not in my body.

## Life after school

Next on my search, was to find out what happened after he left school. With this in mind I used the internet to see if I could contact any of his three brothers. I knew he had a younger brother, Brendan, and made contact with him in 2013. Using the information supplied by Brendan and my own knowledge of Stephen, I think the following may have happened.

After he left school, despite thinking he had done quite well in his A-levels, Stephen decided he did not want to go to university. His parents wanted him to go, but he wanted his independence. He wanted to go abroad.

"I've had enough of school," he told them repeatedly. They didn't listen.

"Just tell us why ... "

Stephen wasn't going to tell them. He'd had enough of people wanting explanations when the Headmaster had called him in, demanding to know whether he too was a homosexual. Though he denied it, he knew what had happened to me and feared ending up like me when he was eighteen the following month. Safer to move on, get right away. Away from the influence of Catholicism.

"You're such a clever boy," his Mum said.

But his Dad had no time for flattery.

"You're being daft, lad. Think of the future."

"Why are you being so obstinate?" This was Mum again.

Stephen didn't answer. Which is when the arguments began.

According to Brendan, there was quite a lot of pressure from his parents for him to go on to further study and a number of heated discussions about this at the time.

Eventually his Dad gave in, saying, "There's this opportunity in Paris."

His father, besides being a teacher, was also a youth worker and managed to find Stephen a job in Paris, working in a hotel kitchen. Being an accomplished French speaker, Stephen would have been happy about the prospect. I can just imagine him in Gay Paree!

A couple of years later, Stephen moved to London to run a restaurant. He lived in Islington and had a girlfriend. Maybe it was that blond lass I rejected in Bradford.

Like me, he worked hard to climb his particular career ladder. He then got a very good job managing a McDonalds in London.

It does not surprise or disappoint me that Stephen had a girlfriend. I am not sure he was ever totally gay, more bisexual really, but from my point of view his sexuality was irrelevant to me. He was there for me when I needed him.

When I told my friends that my images of seeing Stephen die were false, a number of them questioned me. Why, they wanted to know, if Stephen was still alive, I never got to know about it, or met him in Bradford. Well, the fact was, he went off to live in Paris. He was never back in Bradford when I was at school there. No one knew where he went, and no-one talked about him at school. It also explained why his father had told me he didn't know where Stephen was living. He may have genuinely not known.

Stephen very rarely communicated with his family again. He hardly ever went back to Bradford, apart from a couple of days for a wedding in 1976. He effectively disappeared from Bradford more or less permanently. At some point in the late 70's while his family thought he was still working and living in London, he had split with his girlfriend and job and moved to Blackburn to manage a butcher's shop.

I find it remarkable that something must have happened for him to leave a good career in London, to move somewhere far away. It is so similar to my own experience of leaving my well paid Textile Management career to become a railway labourer, then moving to Cumbria. Like me too, though it took me longer to escape, once away from his parents he did not often go back. It seems in the three years prior to his death none of his family knew where he was or what he was doing. So it must have come as an awful shock to his parents when he died in a road accident.

I felt ready to resume my personal quest to find how Stephen actually died. I felt that once I knew for sure, the nightmare images in my mind could at last leave me permanently.

I wondered why there would have been an inquest into his death. Would there be anything in the local press about the crash at the time? I found the details of newspapers held at Blackburn Library and drove down to look through the archives. I found the information about the accident at the time it happened and later on there was a report on the coroner's inquest about his death.

It was disheartening to read the newspaper articles about the accident. The method of his death made me both angry at him and sad for him. He was driving home from a restaurant, late at night, after celebrating his girlfriend's eighteenth birthday. A police car started to follow them, flashing him to stop. Fearing that he had had too much to drink and would fail a breath test, Stephen drove off at high speed. He was chased by the police, until he lost control of his car on a bend and crashed. He died in hospital. It does not mention in the newspaper reports whether his girlfriend was injured. I hope not. At the inquest it was pointed out that his blood alcohol was below the threshold.

I love Stephen with all my heart. I can't help it. In my life he has died twice. I know he is dead, he had been a long time dead to me before he was briefly resurrected. He died in my head, but whether he was just dead in my head or in real life, I still feel love for him. I like that feeling and have no wish to lose it. In the week following, I finally found the tears to grieve properly for Stephen.

CHAPTER TWENTY EIGHT

# Aversion Therapy, the Catholic Version

The horrible thoughts I had after reading my mum's diaries lead me to question why they wouldn't talk to me about being homosexual. Why they would never accept my sexuality.

The priests at my school seemed to have had influence on how I was treated at the mental hospital. Most of what I read about aversion therapy doesn't mention religion. The therapy was carried out by the NHS.

From my research into how the AT was used, it appears to me that each leading psychiatrist in each mental hospital had their own methods of administering the therapy. These ranged from simple talking psychotherapy at one extreme, to chemical castration at the other. What influenced the way these people carried out their own way of doing things?

It would be fairly easy to have a Catholic or Christian doctor carrying out the treatment according to their religious beliefs. The underlings in a mental hospital would have had to follow their lead psychiatrist's way for fear of losing their jobs if they disagreed.

The grumpy psychiatrist who treated me, later famously believed that a serial killer had been told by God to kill women. It's a shame this same doctor couldn't have just asked his God to cure me quietly, instead of torturing me.

How would I have had the knowledge to go to my GP demanding treatment to cure my homosexuality? It was the Headmaster. How did he know where I would be sent for this therapy? If I had been sent to another hospital nearer to my home, the treatment may have been very different. There is no doubt for me that the school had undue influence on where my treatment was carried out.

The fact that the mental hospital was so near to the school makes me feel that over the years, I wasn't the only pupil to have been sent for this brutal treatment by the school. I think diseased St Bede's Grammar School gay boys would always have been sent to the same place no matter where they lived. I wonder too if the Headmaster told all the queer boys not to tell their parents. Then, behind their backs, he made sure their parents knew their sons were diseased homosexuals telling them they could be cured.

I believe that my school's insistence that I start the AT while taking my exams was meant to make me fail them. Then I would have to return to school for the following year, and so the therapy could continue. If they had waited until I had sat my A-levels, there was a probability that I would have passed them and gone to University. Then they couldn't have threatened me with expulsion. It pisses me off that these Catholics decided it was more important for them to 'cure me' than it was for me to pass my exams.

I think it is fair to say that due to their selective readings of the bible, Catholics hate homosexuals. Or should I say, hate homosexuals who have sex with other homosexuals.

Apparently a homosexual can still enter their heaven if they ignore their sexuality completely and become celibate. So, what was the purpose of the aversion therapy supposed to be for me? To turn me straight? Or to turn me celibate?

The following quotes all come from a pamphlet produced in 1999 by the Catholic Medical Association. They have updated their approach a number of times since then. But if this is what they thought in 1999 then, what chance did I have in 1972 when homosexuality was still seen as a curable disease by the medical profession? I must have been seen as a lamb to the slaughter by all those so-called caring adults who were supposed to be looking after my well-being.

> ***http://cathmed.org/resources/position-papers/homosexuality-and-hope***
>
> ***"It should be pointed out that Catholics cannot support forms of therapy which encourage the patients to replace one form of sexual sin with another. (Schwartz 1984) Some therapists, for example, do not consider a patient "cured" until he can comfortably engage in sexual activity with the other sex, even if the patient is not married. (Masters 1979) Others encouraged patients to masturbate using other-sex imagery. (Blitch 1972; Conrad 1976)***
>
> ***For a Catholic with same sex attraction, the goal of therapy should be freedom to live chastely according to one's state in life. Some of those who have struggled with same-sex attractions believe that they are called to a celibate life. They should not be made to feel that they have failed to achieve freedom, because they do not experience desires for the other sex."***

So the goal of my therapy was to turn me celibate. I suppose the fact that after my early twenties I had very little sex ever again, means they were nearly totally successful in their aim. Anxiety played a large part in the AT in that the idea was that a homosexual should be made to feel anxious in the company of men. I still feel uncomfortable in the presence of men, especially those in white coats. This has been commented on occasionally by my GPs when I have been treated by male doctors. All my GPs have been female.

It became clear to me as I read through the above article for the first time that the AT that I underwent was indeed a Catholic, or Christian, (and not an NHS) version of AT. Here are the stated responsibilities set out in the above pamphlet, for the people carrying out my treatment.

> ***"It is most important that Church-related counsellors or support groups be very clear about the nature and genesis of same-sex attraction. This condition is not genetically or biologically determined. This condition is not unchangeable. It is deceitful to counsel individuals experiencing same-sex attractions that it is acceptable to engage in sexual acts provided these occur within the context of a faithful relationship. The teachings of the Catholic Church on sexual morality are explicitly clear and do not allow exceptions. Catholics have a right to know the truth and those working with or for Catholic institutions have an obligation to clearly enunciate that truth."***

For my priests:

> ***It is of paramount importance that priests, when faced with parishioners troubled by same-sex attraction, have access to solid information and genuinely beneficial resources. The priest, however, must do more than simply refer to other agencies.***

***He is in a unique position to provide specific spiritual assistance to those experiencing same-sex attraction. He must, of course, be very sensitive to the intense feelings of insecurity, guilt, shame, anger, frustration, sadness, and even fear in these individuals."***

It amazes me that when I actually needed a little love and understanding they made me feel insecure, guilty, shameful, angry, frustrated, sad and scared. I am not too sure that the priest I confessed my homosexuality to was aware that he had to be sensitive about anything. Maybe his idea was to make sure I was afflicted with all these emotions, so he could come up with a reason to save me.

My doctors:

***"Mental health professionals should familiarize themselves with the works of therapists who have successfully treated persons experiencing same-sex attraction. Because same-sex attraction does not arise from a single cause, different individuals may require different types of treatment. Combining therapy with spiritual healing is also an option that should be considered.***

I am sure the doctors didn't need to familiarise themselves with what they had already been doing for years. But I suppose that as the article was written in 1999, the doctors at that time didn't have carte blanche freedom to do what they liked as they did in 1972.

My teachers:

> ***Teachers in Catholic institutions have a duty to defend the teachings of the Church on sexual morality, to counter false information on same-sex attraction, and to inform at-risk or homosexually involved adolescents that help is available.***

My parents:

> ***When Catholic parents discover that their son or daughter is experiencing same-sex attractions or engaged in homosexual activity, they are often devastated. Afraid for the child's health, happiness, and salvation, parents are usually relieved when informed that same-sex attraction is treatable and preventable.***

According to my mum's diaries it appears that my parents had regular evening meetings with the priests at my school. It seems that some of the meetings took the form of discussion groups always followed by a mass. My mum often remarked how good these meetings were. Knowing my parents, they probably accepted every belief that their priests threw at them. I had no chance. Jeremy had no chance. As soon as young Jeremy admitted to being homosexual, the whole Catholic machine descended upon him, and it treated him in line with its bigoted views.

CHAPTER TWENTY NINE

# Re-connecting

## Dissociation and body memories

Dissociation occurs when events are too painful for the mind to accept. When you dissociate you may have frequent blank spells; have pain for which there is no explanation; feel as if the painful event is happening right now and have nightmares and trouble sleeping. The mind can separate from the body, like an out of body experience.

I think I learnt to dissociate in my teens as a means of escape from having to be where I didn't want to be. When I was trying to control my breathing in the dentist's chair, I escaped into the mountains. When I was at home sitting in the living room with my parents, I managed to escape into a pack of cards. I think I did it to use up the hours when I was alone with my parents.

When I tried to describe how Stephen died, to a psychologist in 1999, my mind went to the place where I thought it happened. In the mental health notes that were taken at the time, the therapist wrote in her notes, 'Got very tense. Shook uncontrollably. Soon he seemed not to tell the story but to actually be there. When I spoke to him I spoke to him there.' The 'there' was where my mind was when I saw my Stephen die in front of me.

The only way I can make sense of this is to believe that I dissociated. I abandoned and betrayed my own body and left it to endure the electric shocks all on its own while my mind was elsewhere. When it returned, what I remember is of wherever my mind took me and not of what was happening in the 'real' world to my body at the time. My body however does remember. The route towards my recovery was to try to re-connect my body memories to my mind. To be whole again.

During my research into body memories and dissociation, I came upon the book by Babette Rothschild, 'The Body Remembers.' I exchanged emails with Babette in which I asked her what she thought of my experiences. She responded saying, "Yes, it is absolutely possible to continue to have body memories of trauma. Sometimes it is helpful to remind oneself of just that, "My body is remembering ______." And then just let the sensations move through. There is no need to focus on the memories, but to allow the sensations to just be. In mindfulness they would say to "sit with it." Acceptance seems to usually work better than trying to "get rid of" or getting angry or frustrated with the recurring sensations."

"Body memories are a common occurrence for trauma survivors. They are an important piece of the healing work. The body can say a lot about the incidents of abuse. It really is impossible to re-create a body memory when there was no memory in the first place. Because of that, body memories can be helpful in breaking through the denial layers of dissociation. The body may remember moments of the abuse that were too emotionally difficult for the survivors to manage, but by truly listening to their bodies, survivors can learn a great deal about their histories."

My body remembers the trauma, and feels the same physical sensations again and again as it "tells the story" of what happened. My mind blocked out the pain and created dissociative walls around the aversion therapy, but my physical body remembers the trauma through cellular memory. It feels the trauma in much the same way as in the original incident and the various physical attitudes occur as if the trauma was happening all over again. The physical pain, shaking, trembling, jerking, physical reactions, intensity, and various body responses happen in a similar fashion as in the original trauma. Unfortunately for me, my body memories appeared separately from intellectual understanding of what happened during the trauma.

I felt intense body pains and had no idea why I was hurting. When my body was trying to get me to remember the electric shocks biting into my forearm, I never connected the pain with the AT. It seems obvious to me now, but not at the time.

The therapeutic goal was to put the various pieces together so that I could work through the process, and heal from the memory as a whole.

The uncontrollable body shaking is the memory my body has of the actual events at the time. I have had many pains in different parts of my body that have never responded to physical help. Some of them have only stopped hurting recently as I began to reconnect them in my mind.

**Oddities**

There are certain things I do, or don't do, that I never thought much about other than the feeling that to carry on doing it, or not doing it, caused me pain. Not a physical pain more a mental one. I find it hard to explain but perhaps the following will make sense.

Shirley told me that however much I was dissociating when I underwent the 'treatment', my physical body will have been traumatised by it, and continues to hold that distress. So we began to work on the unconscious effects my body memory experiences may have had on me without me realising it.

Shirley notices I don't wear a watch. I don't. I haven't worn a watch for over twenty years. She asked me why, I say, "I don't know, I don't like tight things on my wrists." Similarly I do not possess and will not wear any shirts with a buttoned cuff. I mostly roll my sleeves up or wear T-shirts. When I buy thermal vests with tight cuffs I always cut the cuffs off. Shirley asks me, "Why, why do you not want tight things on your wrists." *'Oh shit,'* I finally get it, it is an unconscious effect of the aversion therapy when they fastened my wrists down.

Peace at last one may think, but no, completely the opposite. In the past I would just free the tightness on my wrists, now when I pull my sleeves up I am aware of why I am doing it; reminding me of the electric wrist straps. I think I was better off not knowing.

She notes something else later in another session when she is trying to get me to change my behaviour or try out new interests. She mentions going to the pictures. I tell her that I don't like going to the cinema.

"Why not?"

"I don't know, I just don't like it"

"There it is again" she says, "it reminds you of being in the electric shock chair and looking up at the screen."

When we started analysing my behaviour other aches came to mind; the most evil itch where the electrodes were placed on my forearm. My whole right arm ached from my neck to my wrist. In the past when I knew there was an electric shock coming then my right arm and shoulder would tense up waiting for the pain. I experienced this often during my flashbacks.

I am sure you will understand why I never wear slippers or a dressing gown. For slippers I wear a pair of my old walking boots without the laces. I buy Asian Kurta pyjamas, which are completely different to the standard front opening dressing gowns.

As I grow older, I have a problem with arthritis affecting my joints. Certain arthritic pains occur in the places that were originally affected by the electric shocks, namely my neck, shoulder and wrists. When I get arthritis in these places I flashback. I wish there was a way to stop all this interconnectedness but short of my death I can't think of anything. I hope against hope that sometime in the near future the government will allow assisted dying. I can't bear the thought that I may be trapped in an arthritic body, frequently flashbacking. I wonder if it is possible to dissociate permanently, never to return to my body?

CHAPTER THIRTY

# EMDR and Cognitive dissonance

My therapy took a rest for a couple of years between 2013 and 2015. I still needed to understand why I had dreamt up the vision of seeing Stephen die. I wanted some form of closure. I was again referred for Eye Movement Desensitisation and Reprocessing (EMDR) therapy which is a preferred treatment for people who suffer from Post Traumatic Stress Disorder. EMDR was recommended for me in 1998 but did not receive it. I never knew why.

I must thank Liz for help with the following. Liz was my EMDR therapist in 2015/16. I have a problem with my eyes, which made it difficult to carry out the exercise of flicking them side to side as it made them ache. So she solved that by rhythmically tapping the backs of my hands or my shoulders, depending on my position, as I moved my eyes with them shut.

According to Liz, PTSD tends to create unexpected and sometimes very tenacious symptoms, particularly ones that are expressed as body sensations and behaviours.

EMDR therapy is a strange thing. I am not sure I can really explain it. Liz said that during EMDR things may come up that may or may not be factually accurate. Sometimes the mind processes things 'symbolically,' and sometimes in sorting things through, my mind will generate lots of different scenarios. I won't know until I have finished what is of significance. I struggle anyway with working out what is real and what is a dream.

At the end of every session, Liz would lead me to my 'safe place.' For me this was to imagine I was doing my three-plunge technique into the cold water of Warnscale beck.

During a session Liz would ask me to think of a particular piece of my memory. Then I would close my eyes while she rhythmically tapped the backs of my hands and I would examine any thoughts that came up. She would regularly make me open my eyes and take a deep breath, and talk about what I was feeling, seeing, then I would go back into my mind once more. With this procedure we could go from one part of my memory, connecting to another, in and out, with me just following where my mind took me; structuring my thought processes instead of having them fly all over the place. Liz made it very clear that I was in control and it was up to me whether to proceed with the reprocessing or stop it at any time.

One particular day I wanted to follow what happened in the hospital. I started the journey in the changing room at the hospital where the male nurse told me to strip naked and put on slippers and a dressing gown. I could remember the tone of his voice, as he watched me, he made it obvious that he disliked me.

At this point, I held up this narrative as my mind took me back to the school and my walk up to the mental hospital. I could remember walking along Leylands Lane and at one point I looked at the stone wall alongside the road. I suddenly realized that this was a memory from the first time I walked up to the hospital on my own. I told Liz about this and she said "This is the first time you have mentioned your first visit." I think that maybe when I noticed the stone wall, I was in the now. My mind and body were working together.

One morning, Liz asked me to think of an image of seeing Stephen dead. This induced intense processing which included a lot of physical pain, shaking and confusion. I was re-experiencing electric shocks. We took regular breaks as needed. My picture of Stephen dead became less accessible, as another vision came to me of Stephen getting pissed and falling over in the snow, lying down in it, until I went to him and pulled him upright. The re-processing moved on spontaneously to the aversion therapy. I said, "They wanted me to forget Stephen, but I was determined not to. I was desperate not to lose control but 'they' wanted me to."

"Why did I ever agree to it?" I said and at last, I saw what my younger self had to go through saying, "poor lad." These thoughts moved on from the electric shocks to a man talking, and to me listening to my own recorded voice, then I called a stop to proceedings for that day.

The re-processing continues between sessions. At the beginning of the next session, I told Liz that I find the memory of the road traffic accident harder to think of. I can still see it happening but I know it didn't. I feel sadness, and guilt. I have often felt I was to blame, a murderer, a killer. But I did nothing wrong.

More EMDR processing – again very intense. I had to admit to Dr Grumpy that I was thinking of Stephen and get an electric shock. I'd deny it and still get a shock. I am damned if I do and damned if I don't. I sense the electric shocks are still inside me, a violent pulsating of my diaphragm. I have a deepening insight of how I needed to kill Stephen off in my mind.

At the next session, I said I wanted to lie on the floor. It's when I am lying down that I experience the worst of the internal electric shocks. I thought that if I could force these feelings out into the open I could work on them. The re-processing starts as I begin to experience the electric shocks, shaking, hearing someone talking to me, it's my own voice. I feel that I can't cope ... I can't escape.

Liz makes notes:

> *'Processing very intensive/vivid – he appeared to be physically re-experiencing powerful electric shocks. After thirty minutes, used interweaves to keep him in present, reinforce safety, told him to stop me doing hand taps – after a delay he did manage to. Debriefed in detail – he was surprised by the intensity of processing – reflecting that the aversion therapy was torture.'*

## Cognitive Dissonance

During sessions, Liz sometimes mentioned psychological concepts which may help explain my reaction to the events of 1972. She mentioned Cognitive Dissonance and I asked her to explain it to me.

"It is a long known basic bit of psychology that says: 'If there is pain, effort, or a lot of money involved in something," she says, "Your mind deduces that that thing must be very important.' She says. "For example if something is cheap, people think it is not as special as something more expensive even if it is identical."

I readily agreed with this idea. When I buy paracetamol, or ibuprofen, I only buy those in plain packets which are dirt cheap. The Trade mark named items can cost many times as much for the identical item. I am amazed that people fall for this con-trick. But then I fell for it in a big way myself, so I'd better not criticise anyone else for it.

The doctors at the mental hospital thought they were teaching me to associate loving Stephen with pain so I would stop loving him. But what I have learnt was that lying down and thinking of Stephen, who I loved dearly, leads to pain. What they didn't realise was – by cognitive dissonance – they were persuading me that Stephen must be really, really special. Stephen <u>must</u> be the love of my life if I was tolerating all this pain for him.

When I broke down in the corridor at school in 1972, I was distraught that I was going to lose Stephen in a physical sense. If, instead of a priest going past, a normal teacher or school friend had done so then all I really needed was to be treated gently and maybe hugged. Taken away quietly with no fuss. To talk things through. To have Stephen to hold. By the time I came to exam time I had already reconciled the fact that we would probably not see much of each other again. If we both had passed our exams we were both intending to leave Bradford and go our separate ways. If this position had just been accepted by the adults at school then all would have been well. What the doctors did made my relationship much more important than even I thought it was.

What those responsible for my care did was to assume I was a 'normal' abnormal diseased homosexual. They assumed I would react in the normal way anyone would do regarding pain, i.e. try to avoid it. They have assumed that because it worked on patient A, it will work on patient B. But I am not normal. I have an analytical mind, (cf the snail tale), I can see through things, I don't think like they think I will. They assume that if they make me link pain with Stephen, I will reject him, stop loving him, therefore be cured. That is what is supposed to happen.

They haven't taken into account the strength of my love for Stephen. The psychiatrists wanted me to stop loving him in a physical way. But it was not in the physical sense that I was afraid of losing Stephen. I didn't want to stop loving

Stephen, I wanted to keep my love for him intact. When the doctors told me to think of Stephen, which is what I wanted to do anyway, then they shocked me, verbally abused me, they just assumed the punishment would work but in my case my love for Stephen is far more desirable. The pain becomes a reward for thinking about him. So I associate pain with love and I have got them totally inter-linked. So, as the pain got more intense, then my love for Stephen became more intense to overcome it.

The more pain I received the more valuable to me became my love for Stephen. Using the theory of cognitive dissonance I could not stop the pain.

My mind had to do acrobatics in that:

---- Loving Stephen causes pain.
---- If I am accepting this pain, I must really love him with all of my heart.
---- I want to keep my love for him, but stop the pain.
---- But it's only if I reject Stephen that the pain will stop.

I can't win in this situation, my body feels the pain, but my mind won't give in. My subconscious mind took the only option it had and invented the accident. My brain finds the way by adding just one untruth to a collection of true memories. Stephen dies, the shocking pain stops.

I cannot let myself love someone else and risk getting hurt by losing them too, or have others intervening again. So my mind and body opted for safety and control:

---- I won't love anyone else and get hurt again
---- **I am** controlling the pain
---- I'd rather be in control than let anyone else be.

Unfortunately for me all I have done is exchange one kind of pain for another. The pain of seeing him die means I will continue to love Stephen.

By thinking like this, I had sentenced myself to a lifetime of pain.

CHAPTER THIRTY ONE

# It has always been about that boy

I have a psychological model I work to, my body/brain/mind model. I know when all three are working together I am in control, but I feel that some of the time they do not work together. Over the years I am at my best, happiest, when all three aspects are working together, walking the fells, rock climbing, and especially building dry-stone walls.

I have been stonewalling since I was ten years old. In my childhood, I erected psychological stonewalls to protect my homosexual self, from the hateful people that surrounded me. These walls were consciously built by me knowing exactly what I was doing. They were just like the second ones mentioned below, in that at the beginning, I was not very good at it. Unfortunately for me, the mental wall I built before my first breakdown was in no way strong enough to keep me hidden and safe. I learnt from experience to build my inner wall thicker.

The second kind of stonewalls are those I have built as a professional dry stone waller, about fourteen kilometres by now. Dry-stone walling seems to have a particularly satisfying effect on my mind. When I am walling, my mind is thinking solely about the next stone I need.

There is a saying in dry stone walling work that says, "A good waller never puts a stone down once he/she has picked it up." I believe this saying is responsible for the building of all the worst walls ever built. It is especially hard on learner wallers who can't fathom out where they are supposed to place the horribly shaped stone they have just picked up. The saying is nearly completely wrong. The saying should be "A good waller only ever picks up the stone he/she has decided will fit in next." By already knowing it will fit there will be no need to put it back on the ground.

The third type of wall was a kind I didn't totally discover until 2016. These were the unconscious stonewalls my brain erected in my mind to hide from me the truth of the trauma I was subjected to in that mental hospital in 1972. These walls kept everything hidden until my brain deemed it safe to release the truth. It was only when this third type of wall disintegrated, stone by stone at first, then in a tumult, that I discovered what my brain had been hiding from me.

The adults all those years ago brainwashed me into believing I was not a nice person. I believed it to such an extent that I could not understand why people liked me. How could they like someone who was so vile and diseased?

I have found that I am a strong person mentally; because in the past my younger self went through some awful tortures and discovered a way of living through it all. Somehow imagining that vision of Stephen's accident in a state of extreme distress, gave him something to cling onto. To keep it to himself, which sounds so odd now, but to him then it must have been the only way he could survive the experience. I see now that Stephen was never about pain, all memories of him (apart from one and that was false) are of acceptance and happiness and togetherness.

All the pain, shame and blame comes from the AT and Catholic religion and my treatment by those who knew no better. I also think that the main reason I did not commit suicide, even though I thought about it many times, was that I was keeping the memory of Stephen alive. Loving Stephen, along with his pentagram and our songs, has helped me throughout my life. I am where I am now due to my love for Stephen.

Despite all the pain over the last forty-five years I think I have found a lovely place to be. I have cut myself off all my life, loving Stephen. I am happy living on my own with my dog Timmy. Boady died in 2014. It's strange, I only really feel alone when I am surrounded by people at parties and such, so I try to avoid those. I am a good cook, so I can eat relatively cheaply but very well. I am lucky to have found such a fantastically pleasurable job that dry stone walling is to me. I have lots of lovely friends who are all supportive of me; due to the fact that I actually am a nice man and I have done my best to support all my friends in their own times of need.

## The lost boy

I realise that in my life since I was eighteen there have just been two people. Jerry and Stephen. There is however a lost little soul who I have been ignoring for years and have relegated him to third place behind Stephen. He has been crying out to me from within for many years and I have only just woken up to his presence. There have been lots of nudges, and body memories that have been ignored. He appeared in my nightmare spaceship but I didn't recognise him. The key that I couldn't find. The key that would open the door into my mind so the nightmare could come out and be understood.

He has been within me for all of my life and he is the happy eighteen year old self I left behind when I saw Stephen die. I spent all those years hating him, but he did me no wrong. I must forgive him. I must learn to love him. I must learn to treasure his memories. He is the one Stephen fell in love with. I was just the miserable one who had to live out in the dead zone.

I have always berated my young self for breaking down and bringing everything down on my head. But I see now that the young Jeremy had no chance. Once he had admitted his homosexuality to that priest then the whole Catholic machine swung into action and they took it upon themselves to try to cure what they saw as a diseased evil boy.

I should be saying to my younger self, "Well done Jeremy, you were in an impossible situation that you should not have been put in; you did what you could to survive."

Now I can say to my whole self: "I am safe now and in control of my life, I wasn't then, so I don't need to hide from the truth now"

In 1998 when my mum found out I was depressed, she asked me, "Is it about that boy?" This has always bugged me because I never ever told her about Stephen.

I don't remember how I answered then, but the answer now would be, "Yes mum, it has always been about that boy." Not Stephen though, just young Jeremy.

# Coda

As I started to write my story, I had no idea where it would take me. It was meant to be a mental health exercise to try to understand my life. I found it hard to find the words to express my feelings, but I kept working on it. Over the years, it developed from a personal story into a book I hope will help other gay men, who experienced the hatred of a society that deemed us diseased and curable. I hope that my book will go a little way to righting the wrongs of the past, and reduce the risk of it happening again in this country. I hope it will go some way to deter all those countries of the world where the practice of conversion therapy still happen.

All through the last seven years, I have been seeking healing for myself, never giving up. Doggedly following wherever I needed to go, to find the answers. Not knowing where I would end up. I said to someone a long time ago that I had given up the idea of killing myself because, "I wanted to find out what happened next."

Well, what happened next, I couldn't have dreamed of.

My biggest achievement, apart from staying alive, happened in October 2017.

To advertise my book I gave an interview to Patrick Strudwick of LGBT Buzzfeed. The article he created lead to the Royal College of Psychiatry releasing the following statement, part of which states:

*"There are no words that can repair the damage done to anyone who has ever been deemed 'mentally unwell' simply for loving a person of the same sex. For those who were then 'treated' using non-evidence based procedures by mental health professionals up until as late as the 1970s, the trauma of such experiences can never be erased.*

*The injustice of those within the LGB community who were treated as mentally unwell due to their sexual orientation alone is keenly felt by mental health professionals.*

*It is with profound regret that we hear of the lifelong impact that treatments such as 'aversion therapy' had on Jeremy Gavins and others."*

**Professor Wendy Burn, President of the Royal College of Psychiatry**
The full statement can be seen on the Royal College of Psychiatry website.

# Acknowledgements

A huge thank you to:

All my closest friends for believing in me when I didn't believe in myself: Eileen Palmer, Jim Whitling, Julie Lee, Janet Packwood, Alison Boon for getting me to write letters, John and Debbie, a Scottish puffin, Charlotte, Tim, Matthew and Lucy, Malcolm Judge, Vickie Lambert, Lou Neill, Shaun and Sam, Andrew Wright and posthumously, Stuart Raistrick. All my lovely nieces.

The barman in the Newfield Inn one night in 1975. All those car drivers who managed to miss me when I staggered around drunk. My two four legged friends who loved me unconditionally, Boady and Timmy.

Everyone at The Literary Consultancy, especially Aki Schilz and Sybil Ruth

All the members of the Ulverston Writers Group, without whose editorial help this book would never have been finished and my proofreader Vanessa Rengger, and cover designer Sarah Cowan.

Patrick Strudwick of Buzzfeed, for putting my story online on 30 September 2017 and in getting the Royal College of Psychiatry to issue the historic statement on Monday 16 October 2017.

Victoria Derbyshire for inviting me onto her BBC2 programme on Tuesday 17 October 2017

All those who have helped keep me mentally, physically and spiritually strong especially: Sarah Adams, Shirley Walker, Liz Bolt, Jane Alexander and Helen Rice.